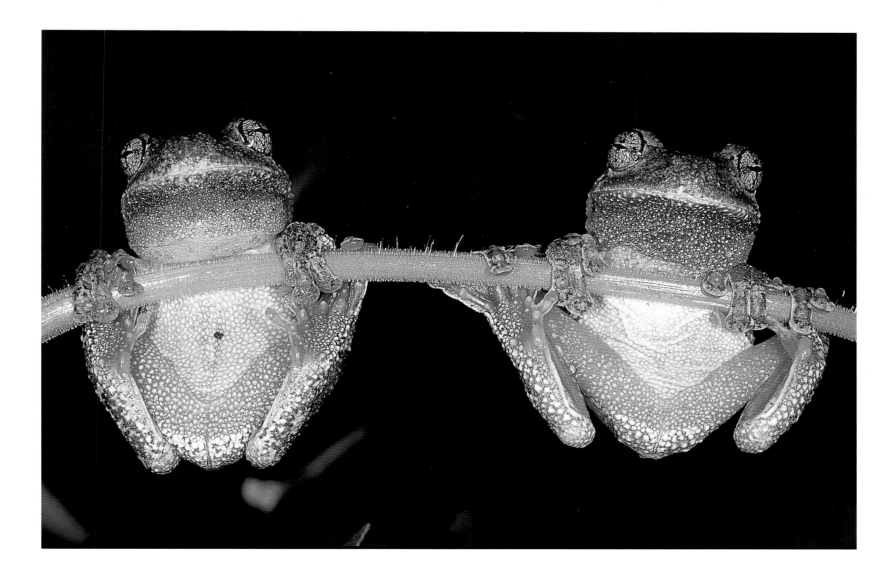

*Ask a toad what is beauty;
. . . he will answer that it is the female
with two great round eyes coming out
of her little head, her flat mouth, her
yellow belly, and brown back.
—Voltaire*

Frogs

Text by David Badger

Photography by John Netherton

CRESTLINE

Dedication

For my wife, Sherry, and son, Jeffrey, whose patience, good humor,
and support made this endeavor possible. —D.B.

For my loving wife, Judy, and my wonderful children, Jason, Joshua,
Erich, Joshua, and Evan. —J.N.

Acknowledgments

The authors wish to express their gratitude to the following for their assistance with this book:

Eric Anderson; Mike Carlton, Radnor Lake State Natural Area; Jim and Jamie R. Clark; Dr. Joseph T. Collins, Center for North American Amphibians and Reptiles; Eastman Kodak; Jerry Gingerich; Shelly Graham; Joseph Hewgley, Public Library of Nashville and Davidson County; Rob Hoffman; Catesby Jones; Mark Kays; Betty McFall, Todd Library, Middle Tennessee State University; Louise Mesa, Frog Fantasies Museum; Dr. Brian Miller, Department of Biology, Middle Tennessee State University; Nikon Inc.; Alan Resetar, Field Museum of Natural History; Gary M. Stolz; Tennessee Reptile and Amphibian Society; Lex Thomas; Dr. James L. Vial, Declining Amphibian Populations Task Force; Wisconsin Department of Natural Resources; and Sam and Winston.

Asian leaf frog

This edition published in 2011 by CRESTLINE a division of BOOK SALES, INC.
276 Fifth Avenue, Suite 206, New York, New York 10001 USA

This edition published by arrangement with Voyageur Press,
an imprint of MBI Publishing Company

First published in 1995 by Voyageur Press, an imprint of MBI Publishing Company,
400 First Avenue North, Suite 300, Minneapolis, Minnesota, 55401

Edited by Michael Dregni
Designed by Kathryn Mallien
Printed in China

ISBN-13: 978-0-7858-2843-3

10 9 8 7 6 5 4 3 2 1

On the frontispiece: Gray tree frogs.
On the title pages, large photo: In the Deep South, frogs remain active year-round in many swamps, where warm temperatures
make hibernation unnecessary. The lusty serenades of male pig frogs, bronze frogs, chorus frogs, and tree frogs advertising for
mates from the swampy waters, shores, and moss-draped cypress trees can be heard at night from distances of a mile or more.
On the title pages, small photo: American toad.
On page 144: Dart-poison frog (Dendrobates azureus).

Contents

Glass tree frog

Introduction

"WELL, I DON'T SEE NO P'INTS ABOUT THAT FROG THAT'S ANY BETTER'N ANY OTHER FROG."

That sentiment, voiced by a compulsive gambler in Mark Twain's acclaimed short story "The Celebrated Jumping Frog of Calaveras County," first appeared in a New York literary journal in 1865. Of course, that was before color photography was invented—and before nature photographers like John Netherton began to distill the beauty of the natural world through their artistic images.

Doubtless, John would rather sidestep the issue of whether one frog's "p'ints" are better than those of any other, yet his vast portfolio of photographs suggests that some p'ints (and, for that matter, some species) *are* more distinctive or remarkable than others.

For more than twenty-five years now, John has been taking photographs of frogs and toads—some exotic, others familiar—on his regular pilgrimages to the Everglades, Great Smoky Mountains, Big South Fork, northern woodlands, southwestern deserts, and abroad. While herons and egrets, or landscapes and abstracts, were often foremost on his mind, other fauna and flora caught his eye as well, whether he was waist-deep in duckweed in a bald cypress swamp or braced precariously on a mountain overlook.

In the fall of 1993, after completing a book about North American wading birds, *At the Water's Edge* (Voyageur Press), John decided to pursue his interest in frogs. It was time, he felt, to showcase the beauty of these enchanting creatures, whose secrecy and nocturnal behavior all too often cause them to be overlooked. And so was born the idea for a book about these unsung but highly vocal musicians of the night.

Red-eyed tree frog
The red-eyed tree frog of Central America is a gentle-looking, highly photogenic species that has been featured on countless magazine covers and T-shirts around the world. These slender frogs sleep by day, folding in their brightly colored legs to blend in with surrounding foliage; as dusk approaches, they open their enormous eyes, stretch their limbs, and stalk insect prey in the rain forest canopy.

*I believe
a leaf of grass is no less than
the journey-work of the stars,
And the pismire is equally perfect,
and a grain of sand,
and the egg of the wren,
And the tree toad is
a chef-d'oeuvre for the highest,
And the running blackberry would
adorn the parlours of heaven.
—Walt Whitman,
"Song of Myself," 1855*

Dart-poison frog
Scientists discover new species of dart-poison frogs in the rain forests of Central and South America every year. Some species, such as this Epipedobates trivittatus, *find bromeliads ideal sites for laying their eggs.*

My own involvement in this project came about as the result of two chance events. Almost twenty years ago, I saw—and coveted—a color photograph published in the glossy Sunday-magazine section of a Nashville newspaper. The photograph portrayed the head of a green snake with its tongue extended—the spitting image of a snake I had caught many years earlier when I was growing up in Illinois. Walking to school one day, I spotted this snake sunning himself in an alley; I scooped him up and carried him off to my fourth-grade class, where the teacher placed him in a terrarium. My classmates and I admired that snake for weeks, until, as a group, we escorted him to a nearby park and reluctantly set him free.

That chance encounter with a suburban green snake sparked my early interest in reptiles and amphibians, an interest that was to continue over the years—not just on the homefront, where my mother tolerated the green snakes I periodically ordered from a snake farm in Louisiana (plus an assortment of newts, lizards, turtles, and one short-lived African clawed frog), but also at a Wisconsin summer camp, where I was a nature counselor for five summers.

After briefly considering a career in veterinary medicine, I elected to pursue journalism instead (less bloody) and eventually moved to Nashville to teach writing. But memories of that bygone serpent flooded back when I saw the photograph in the Sunday *Tennessean;* little did I suspect that a sun-worshipping green snake from the North Shore of Chicago would predestine my introduction to, and later friendship with, a gifted nature photographer who had an eye for interesting reptiles.

And, it turned out, for frogs.

John and I first "met" when I phoned him to ask whether I could purchase an enlargement of the photograph. He agreed and immediately ordered a print from an out-of-state lab. But its delivery was delayed for months (someone at the lab apparently mislaid the picture), and, in the interim, John felt so terrible that he offered to shoot some pictures for a campus magazine I was editing. By the time the ill-starred snake photo finally turned up, John and I had become friends—and had begun our first collaboration.

That first undertaking, however, was hardly typical; for subsequent projects, John not only furnished the photographs, he also produced the prose, which I would edit prior to final publication.

Until *Frogs.*

This time, after discussing his latest book idea, John surprised me by asking whether I would like to write it. I mulled over this offer. My lack of proper herpetological credentials could be a problem, I said, and I didn't wish to write a field guide, because there were already excellent reference volumes available.

"Don't worry," John laughed; "there's too many species for that anyway." What he had in mind, he said, was a *representative* selection, showcasing some of the more interesting and colorful frogs and toads of the world.

The book would have to be nontechnical and directed toward a general audience, I said, and it would have to be more "accessible" (I meant more "readable") than most articles published in scholarly journals and zoological literature.

"Fine," John replied, "that's your problem. You just write the text, and I'll take the pictures."

The challenge, we found, was to produce something fresh; fortunately for me, John's body of work offered ample inspiration. Through the eloquence of his spectacular color images, John convinced me that frogs deserved a larger audience. I was awed by the beauty of the tropical dart-poison frogs he had photographed, tantalized by the matchstick limbs and delicate toepads of the tree frogs, and struck by the vivid eye colors and pupils of the toads. Later, after we went out together at night to listen to frog choruses performing their mating calls and raspy rain calls, I was hooked.

John's growing portfolio of frog photographs—portraits of individual specimens, as well as behavioral and natural-habitat shots—might, I felt, encourage the public to better appreciate these little-seen amphibians and perhaps even restore some sense of balance relative to their better-known mammalian, avian, and reptilian counterparts.

We were aware, however, that frogs and toads were a risky subject for a book. Even today, some people still think of amphibians as slimy, ugly, disgusting creatures that creep around in foul-smelling swamps and give warts to humans. This, of course, is utter nonsense. As naturalist Joseph Wood Krutch once put it: "Frogs are beautiful in their own fashion and ask only that we enlarge our conception of beauty to include one more of nature's many kinds. They are as triumphantly *what* they are as man has ever succeeded in being. . . . They are the perfect embodiment of frogginess both outwardly and inwardly . . . not shadows of an ideal but the ideal itself."

Still, frogs aren't just another pretty face—they're also of enormous economic value to humans, since they devour huge quantities of insects and serve as a critical link in the food chain. Unfortunately, they are also far worse off today than ever before. In the United States and elsewhere,

humans threaten frogs' dual existence on land and in the water with massive habitat destruction, water pollution, pesticides and herbicides, overcollection, pulverization by motor vehicles, and even egg-damaging ultraviolet radiation that enters the atmosphere through holes in the ozone layer.

Fortunately, there is a growing awareness that frogs are at risk, and many people are endeavoring to do something about it. Herpetologists have alerted their fellow scientists about declining amphibian populations in the United States and abroad. Environmental groups have made rain forest destruction in Central and South America an international concern. Conservationists have challenged the draining of wetlands and the damming and diverting of rivers. Countries have banned the export of indigenous amphibians at peril. And mainstream media have joined scholarly journals and science magazines in reporting about the plight of frogs and toads.

Today, there is evidence that the public is rallying around these tiny nighttime vocalists. Rain-forest coalitions have virtually adopted the red-eyed tree frog as their symbol. Merchandisers have awakened to frogs' popularity and now feature them on T-shirts, sweatshirts, boxer shorts, ties, hats, boots, umbrellas, shower curtains, mugs, plates, foreign postage stamps, greeting cards, weathervanes, and mailboxes. Frog toys are a big hit with youngsters; gardeners adorn their yards with frog statuary made of concrete, clay, and dried manure; and women and men sport frog earrings, pins, pendants, rings, cufflinks, and other jewelry.

High school and college biology classes are embracing software that makes dissecting dead frogs a thing of the past. The Frog's Leap Vineyard in St. Helena,

Frogs are beautiful in their own fashion and ask only that we enlarge our conception of beauty to include one more of nature's many kinds. They are as triumphantly what they are as man has ever succeeded in being. . . . They are the perfect embodiment of frogginess both outwardly and inwardly . . . not shadows of an ideal but the ideal itself.
—Naturalist Joseph Wood Krutch, "The Contemplative Toad" in The Desert Year, 1952

Dart-poison frog
The Colombian dart-poison frog Dendrobates lehmanni *has wide alternating red-and-black or red-and-white bands across its body. The call of the male reportedly resembles a duck quacking.*

Frogs are showing their true colors, as it were, and imprinting themselves on the public consciousness. They pop up periodically in music; they command starring roles in motion pictures and cartoons; they promote Budweiser beer in TV commercials; they are featured on the covers of magazines; and they are the subject of no less than five calendars for 1995—surely a barometer of sorts indicating new heights of popularity.

Of course, frogs have entertained readers for centuries. Long before Mark Twain's "The Celebrated Jumping Frog of Calaveras County" extolled the virtues of a "gifted" California frog named Dan'l Webster, these animals were featured in folklore and fables, such as those by Aesop (whose tales probably were based on Egyptian stories predating his own by eight hundred to one thousand years). In the Old Testament, the Egyptian pharaoh encounters a plague of frogs in the Book of Exodus, and frogs materialize in other Biblical passages as well. Aristophanes staged his satiric production of *Frogs* in 405 B.C.; Izaak Walton touted frogs (chiefly as bait) in his classic work *The Compleat Angler*; Nathaniel Hawthorne wrote a story called "Mrs. Bullfrog"; Emily Dickinson composed poems about frogs; John Steinbeck depicted a frenzied frog hunt in *Cannery Row*; and, as recently as the fall of 1994, two popular books featured frogs in their titles: Tom Robbins' *Half Asleep in Frog Pajamas* and Lorrie Moore's *Who Will Run the Frog Hospital?*

What better time, then, to champion the humble frog than the present?

For this book, we assembled a portfolio of John's photographs of frogs and toads from around the world—from North and South America, Africa, Australia, Europe, and Asia. Accompanying the photos is text emphasizing characteristics

California, produces a wine so popular that many stores can't keep it in stock—and donates profits to a newsletter about threatened amphibians. The Worldwide Fair Play for Frogs Committee leaps into controversies and skewers bureaucrats who victimize frogs. Peace Frogs sells merchandise with its international frog logo in Washington, D.C., and more than a dozen other cities and contributes money to charity. And the Frog Fantasies Museum in Eureka Springs, Arkansas, attracts tourists from all over the world with an exhibition of more than six thousand frog items.

that make these species interesting or unique. Although scientific names have been included, this is strictly for clarity's sake, since debate still rages within taxonomic circles and some species still lack common names (or boast more than one). Other chapters provide information about frog behavior and physical characteristics, the curious relationship between frogs and people, and the alarming plight of frog and toad populations whose numbers are in decline.

While reviewing recent books and articles for this text, I was surprised to discover that a great deal of today's scientific literature emphasizes the experimental side of biological research. Arthur Bragg, in his milestone study of spadefoot toads *Gnomes of the Night*, notes that experimental research came to dominate biological literature around the turn of the century, and other authors confirm this. For the general reader, however, these studies too often are mired in impenetrable statistics and scientific jargon at the expense of robust description, personal anecdote, and lucid prose.

Accordingly, I have gone back to some older sources, including books long out of print, that I felt presented material in a more satisfying fashion. I am particularly indebted to a trio of authors—Mary C. Dickerson, Doris Cochran, and Olive Goin—whose contributions to herpetological literature clearly demonstrate that not all studies of frogs and toads need be dry or colorless.

While many of the frogs and toads included in this book will be recognized immediately by readers, others may be new. This is understandable, given the enormous number of species worldwide. Of course, not every frog needs to be a celebrity to be enjoyed or appreciated, but a higher profile and greater public respect might prove useful, given the gravity of the current environmental situation.

When Mark Twain's "Jumping Frog" story was first published, the author was elated to find that even a lowly frog could attain what he called "wide celebrity" (he did grouse, however, that "it was only the frog that was celebrated. It wasn't I. I was still an obscurity"). Clearly, some "p'ints" about Twain's frog were special after all. Today, the photographs of John Netherton confirm that frogs remain special even as we confront the ecological uncertainties of the twenty-first century.

"Ho, ho!" he said to himself as he marched along with his chin in the air, "what a clever Toad I am! There is surely no animal equal to me for cleverness in the whole world!"
—Kenneth Grahame, The Wind in the Willows, 1908

Barking tree frogs
Barking tree frogs can change color—from bright green to yellow, gray, or brown—with amazing speed.

Frogs and People

"MAYBE YOU UNDERSTAND FROGS," MARK TWAIN MUSED IN HIS FAMOUS STORY, "THE CELEBRATED Jumping Frog of Calaveras County," "and maybe you don't understand 'em; maybe you've had experience, and maybe you an't only a amature."

Most of us, of course, are "amatures" when it comes to frogs, yet even the most reclusive and squeamish human beings have probably encountered a frog or toad somewhere—in a garden, near a pond, in the woods, in a classroom, or at the zoo.

"Frogs are so common and so widely distributed that most of us make their acquaintance at an early age," herpetologist Charles Bogert once observed. "If they were rare creatures, or confined to some distant outpost, we might well look upon them as marvels of nature.

"In many respects," he added, "that is just what they are."

Bogert was right: Frogs *are* marvels of nature—tailless, moist-skinned vertebrates without hair, feathers, or scales that live on land and/or in the water. Like their fellow taxonomic "class" mates—the salamanders, newts, sirens, and caecilians—they acquired the name amphibian "not because they go in and out of the water like an 'amphibian' airplane," Archie Carr and Coleman Goin explain, "but because most of them begin life as aquatic larvae or tadpoles and later change shape and go out on land to live." This unusual ability of theirs to metamorphose (transform physically) has attracted man's interest for centuries. More recently, scientists have discovered that some frogs can even switch their gender.

*Frogs in the marsh mud
drone their old lament.
—Virgil, Georgics*

Green tree frog
The loud, raspy voice of the green tree frog creates such a racket that it often keeps human neighbors awake at night during the spring and summer mating season. These frogs breed in standing water and swamps, where pitcher plants produce a fragrance that attracts insects—and, in turn, hungry tree frogs.

> Then the Lord said to Moses, "Go to Pharaoh and say to him, 'This is what the Lord says: Let my people go, so that they may worship me. If you refuse to let them go, I will plague your whole country with frogs. The Nile will teem with frogs. They will come up into your palace and your bedroom and onto your bed, into the houses of your officials and on your people, and into your ovens and kneading troughs. The frogs will go up on you and your people and all your officials.'"
> —Exodus 8:1-4

*T*he brachycephalid *Psyllophryne didactyla* of Brazil is the world's smallest frog at approximately 0.39 inch (10 mm).

"I wouldn't be surprised if sex change is found in more amphibians," biologist Robert R. Warner told *Science News* in 1990 after he found that female African reed frogs had changed their sex in the laboratory. "We just have to keep looking." As readers and moviegoers may recall, it is gender transformation in the frog DNA mixed with dinosaur DNA in Michael Crichton's *Jurassic Park* that permits the genetically engineered female velociraptors and compys to breed and run amok.

Frogs and toads fascinate their human observers for many reasons. For one thing, frogs sport a dazzling array of colors and markings—some for camouflage, others to warn away predators. Adults also vary a good deal in size, from Brazil's tiny brachycephalid *Psyllophryne didactyla* (approximately 0.39 inch or 10 mm) to the West African goliath frog (approximately 15.50 inches or 388 mm), and they exhibit similar diversity in body shape, from the slender tree frogs and narrow-waisted "true frogs" to the stout-bodied toads and buxom burrowing frogs. Like reptiles and fish, they are cold-blooded (or ectothermic), which means their body temperature varies with the external temperature; amazingly, some species have developed strategies to survive in the subzero Arctic as well as in hot, arid deserts.

They also produce astonishing music, which paleontologist Robert Bakker calls "the richest sonic symphonies in today's ecosystem." During the Middle Ages, servants were employed "for the sole purpose of keeping the noise down by beating the pond, throwing stones into the water, or otherwise disturbing the frogs," Hans Gadow reports; European monks sometimes exorcised frogs "in order not to be disturbed in their vigils." During the French and Indian Wars in America, the

village of Windham, Connecticut, was awakened one night by the sound of an approaching army. "Old and young, male and female, fled naked from their beds," the Rev. Samuel Peters wrote in 1781; "the men, after a flight of half a mile . . . sent a triumvirate to capitulate with the supposed French and Indians. . . . At length, they discovered that the dreaded inimical army was an army of thirsty frogs going to the river for a little water."

Platoons of these nocturnal pilgrims croon in virtually every corner of the world, to the delight and consternation of attending humans. According to Archie Carr, irate Floridians occasionally contact university zoologists to complain about the hideous din raised by frogs on summer nights. "I can't say I actually sympathize with those people," Carr reflects. "There is more intellectual reward in a rousing frog chorus than in much of television, but it is good to hear and be heard by your family at times, and sleep is to be cherished always."

Over the centuries, human beings have attached countless labels to frogs and toads, many of them inaccurate or unfair. In his thirteenth-century opus *Man and the Beasts*, Albert Magnus called the *Rana* (Latin for "frog") a "four-legged worm." Five centuries later, when the Swedish scientist Carolus Linnaeus coined the term *Amphibia* for use in his new system of nomenclature, he characterized the creatures as "foul and loathsome" and "a very queer assembly."

"These animals," he declared, "are abhorrent because of their cold body, pale color, cartilaginous skeleton, filthy skin, fierce aspect, calculating eye, offensive smell, harsh voice, squalid habitation, and terrible venom; and so their Creator has not exerted his powers to make many of them."

The frog pool was square. . . . There were frogs there all right, thousands of them. Their voices beat the night, they boomed and barked and croaked and rattled. They sang to the stars, to the waning moon, to the waving grasses. They bellowed love songs and challenges. The men crept through the darkness toward the pool. . . . As they drew quietly near, the frogs heard them coming. . . . During the millennia that frogs and men have lived in the same world, it is probable that men have hunted frogs. And during that time a pattern of hunt and parry has developed. The man with net or bow or lance or gun creeps noiselessly, as he thinks, toward the frog. The pattern requires that the frog sit still, sit very still and wait. The rules of the game require the frog to wait until the final flicker of a second, when the net is descending, when the lance is in the air, when the finger squeezes the trigger, then the frog jumps, plops into the water, swims to the bottom and waits until the man goes away. That is the way it is done, the way it has always been done. Frogs have every right to expect it will always be done that way.
—John Steinbeck, Cannery Row, 1945

Glass large-eyed frog
The glass large-eyed frog lives close to water in the tropical forests and plains of East Africa. This species, recognized by its large head and enormous eyes, avoids exposing its lighter underside during the day, drawing in its legs and assuming an elliptical shape that resembles the leaves it sleeps on.

*A*mphibians have flourished on planet Earth for 350 million years.

Dart-poison frog

The skin secretions of dart-poison frogs have fascinated European and American scientists for nearly two centuries. The toxins of some species, such as this blue dart-poison frog (Dendrobates azureus), may one day provide medical breakthroughs as heart stimulants, muscle relaxants, and anesthetics. In nature, animals clad in blue are quite rare; this diurnal (day-active) female sports bright hues to warn enemies of her deadly skin secretions.

In that last bit of theological twaddle, Linnaeus was sorely mistaken. At last count, approximately 3,975 different species of frogs and toads have been identified worldwide, according to Dr. Joseph T. Collins of the Center for North American Amphibians and Reptiles, and every year another one or two dozen are discovered. ("We're not living in the Age of Mammals," Bakker jokes, "we're living in the Age of Frogs.")

Amphibians have flourished on this planet for roughly 350 million years, and—if humanity doesn't succeed in obliterating their habitats or wiping them out with its lethal store of pesticides and pollutants—they should still be around for many more to come. Fossilized remains of the earliest frogs date back some 150 million years to the Jurassic Period, and a frog found preserved in amber in the Dominican Republic is believed to be 30 million to 40 million years old.

Frogs and toads are "notorious for their lack of definitive external characters," herpetologist William Duellman points out, and taxonomists have struggled for years to assign and standardize scientific names for individual species. Many people, in fact, may be surprised to learn that all toads are frogs. In general, however, the term "toad" is applied to species with squat bodies, short hind legs, little webbing on the feet, parotoid glands behind the eyes, and dry, warty skin. (The chest cartilage of toads differs, too, but this distinction is muddled by the Darwin's frog, which combines aspects of both varieties.)

By whatever name, these amphibians have beguiled and bedeviled humanity since time immemorial. Primitive people discovered early on that frogs are tasty, and cultures around the globe have been devouring frog legs in obscene quantities ever since. (The United States alone imports over 1.25 million pounds or 562,500 kg each year from Bangladesh, Southeast Asia, Australia, and New Zealand.)

"No more succulent dish, no greater delicacy is obtainable than fresh frog legs," the Florida Department of Agriculture once crowed. The appeal of frog meat, which is low in fat and carbohydrates and tastes rather like chicken, "is due to its delicacy and palatability," the Floridians proclaimed, "which places it in the first rank of epicurean luxuries."

In fact, an entire nation of connoisseurs was alleged to be so enamored of the flavor of this meat that its citizens came to be known—contemptuously—as "frogs." Calling a Frenchman a "frog" (short for "frog-eater") has long been a popular form of abuse; the label caught on during World War I, some language experts say, when American GIs picked up the word

from British soldiers. In truth, however, the term dates back much further.

"*Frog*," John Farmer and W.E. Henley explain in their pre-World War I dictionary of slang, formerly referred to "a Parisian, the shield of whose city bore three toads, while the quaggy state of the streets gave point to a jest common at Versailles before 1791: *Qu'en disent les grenouilles?* i.e., 'What do the frogs [the people of Paris] say?'" Curiously, these same three toads may also explain the origin of the fleur-de-lis, which first appeared as a symbol of French sovereignty on the royal seal of Louis VII. Some heraldry experts see the fleur-de-lis as originally a flower, says authority Whitney Smith, "others a weapon, still others a frog, such as those appearing in the flag from a tapestry in the Cathedral of Reims."

Whether the fleur-de-lis is a lily or a toad, there is no mistaking the French appetite for frogs. Chef Paul Bocuse includes four recipes for preparing frog legs in his definitive *French Cooking*, and culinary expert Anne Willan explains in *La France Gastronomique* that intense French demand is met by "sacks of live frogs [that] arrive in summer from Turkey by truck and in winter from Egypt by air."

A whopping fifty different recipes appear in *Bullfrog Farming and Frogging in Florida*, including Bullfrog Salad, Bullfrog Pot Pie, Bullfrog à la King, Bullfrog Short Cakes, Bullfrog Omelet, Bullfrog Clubhouse Sandwich, and French Toasted Bullfrog Meat.

Significantly, the decline of at least one native species—the California red-legged frog—can be attributed to "Francophilism" in San Francisco following the California Gold Rush. "As the century wore on, and Californians tired of their state's international reputation for ruggedness and violence," Kathryn Phillips

Old pond
Frog jumps in
The sound of water.
—Basho

Primitive people discovered that frogs are tasty, and cultures around the globe have devoured frog legs ever since; the United States imports over 1.25 million pounds (562,500 kg) of frog legs annually.

Pygmy banana frog
The pygmy banana frog of tropical Africa may be tiny, but it is a dynamic jumper. These nocturnal frogs spend the day concealed in hollow logs or clinging to the leaves of banana trees and other vegetation near water.

*T*he earliest fossilized remains of frogs date back 150 million years to the Jurassic Period.

writes in *Tracking the Vanishing Frogs*, "all things French became popular, especially French cuisine." Nearly 120,000 frogs were speared for California restaurant consumption in 1895 alone, triggering not only the decline of the local red-legged population but also the importation of the state's first bullfrogs—which, in turn, began to prey on local frogs.

While diners were savoring the succulent hind legs of frogs in San Francisco and elsewhere (notably the American South, where hefty bullfrogs and pig frogs were readily available), their children were encountering frogs in literature. Aesop's fables featured these creatures, as did German fairy tales ("The Frog Prince") and Russian folktales ("The Frog Princess," "The King of the Toads"). So too did Joel Chandler Harris' *Legends of the Old Plantation*, with Brer Bull-Frog; Beatrix Potter's *The Tale of Mr. Jeremy Fisher*, the story of a frog with no flair for fishing; Kenneth

Grahame's *The Wind in the Willows*, which introduced the clever, conceited, and headstrong Mr. Toad; Thornton W. Burgess' tales with Grandfather Frog and Old Mr. Toad; and scores of others.

More recently, frogs have charmed young readers in Susan Colling's *Frogmorton* (illustrated by Ernest H. Shepard, who also drew Mr. Toad); Arnold Lobel's *Frog and Toad Are Friends* and its sequels; Jim Smith's *Frog Band* books; Donald Elliott's *Frogs and the Ballet*; Steven Kellogg's *The Mysterious Tadpole*; Jane Yolan's *Commander Toad in Space*; various works by David McPhail; and David Wiesner's 1991 Caldecott Medal–winning *Tuesday*.

On the motion-picture screen, long before director George McCowan cast a bizarre assortment of amphibians as the "heroes" of his 1972 ecological horror film *Frogs* (and before the popular children's videos "Frog" and its sequel, "Frogs"), theatrical cartoons headlined frogs and toads. When Ub Iwerks, the co-creator of Mickey Mouse, got into a dispute with Walt Disney, he left to produce and direct three dozen "Flip the Frog" cartoons. Chuck Jones, who worked with Iwerks at Flip the Frog Productions, animated the cult favorite "One Froggy Evening" for Warner Bros. And the "Tijuana Toads" (later the "Texas Toads") co-starred a corpulent toad and his skinny apprentice in seventeen Laurel-and-Hardyesque cartoons. Meanwhile, on television, Jim Henson's Muppet creation Kermit the Frog captivated audiences of all ages and went on to international stardom.

Frogs regularly pop up in popular music, too. "Froggy Went a Courtin' " was an English folksong; James Scott's "Frog Legs Rag" was a ragtime hit in 1906; and such numbers as "Frolic of the Frogs," "Frog Hop," "Frog Tongue Stomp,"

"Frogtown Blues," the Doors' "Peace Frog," and Three Dog Night's "Joy to the World" ("Jeremiah was a bullfrog . . . ") have all rocked America at one time or another.

Many of the world's superstitions, myths, and folktales involve frogs and toads. In ancient Egypt, where the frog was a symbol of female fertility, Egyptian women wore gold amulets with depictions of frogs to attract the "favours of fruitfulness," according to froglore authority Gerald Donaldson. Frogs were also Egyptian symbols of water and primordial slime, and representations of four of the eight gods responsible for the creation of the world bore the heads of frogs. In the Temple of Thebes, embalmed frogs were laid to rest beside human mummies.

Frogs are associated with weather in many ancient cultures—a logical connection, since their rain calls often precede showers or storms. In Sanskrit, the word for "frog" also means "cloud"—and frogs were said to personify the thunder in the sky. Native Americans and Australian aborigines regarded the croaking of the frog as a portent of rain, and Europeans and Americans have claimed that frogs, fish, and other animals have been dumped on their lawns and streets by "inexplicable" rains. (In 1882, for example, witnesses insisted they saw frogs emerge from hailstones in Iowa.)

Other superstitions associate frogs with personal misfortunes. "If the first frog that you see in the spring is sitting on dry ground," folklorists Cora Daniels and C.M. Stevans wrote nearly one hundred years ago, "it signifies that during the same year you will shed as many tears as the frog would require to swim away in." If, however, the first frog of spring jumps into water, "you will experience misfortune all that year." Should the first "hoptoad" of spring jump toward you, "you will have many friends; but if it is going from you, you will lose some." Toads in particular are frequently associated with evil, and sometimes they assume the guise of a demon or devil.

In Japan, however, frogs are a sign of good luck: Bullfrogs are the descendants of a mighty forebear who could suck all the mosquitoes out of a room in a single breath. Other legends about frogs and toads are widespread throughout the Orient, particularly one suggesting that a wrinkled, warty toad is really an ugly old man or a wise guru. The Chinese, according to toad expert Robert De Graaff, regard the toad as one of the "five poisons" or negative forces of *yin*, and see a "toad in the moon" rather than a man. When this moon-toad "attempts to swallow the moon itself," the result is an eclipse.

In recent centuries, the relationship between frogs and people has achieved its greatest distinction in the world of science (or, as G.K. Noble once put it, in "their martyrdom to science"). The Italian physicist Luigi Galvani discovered muscles could be stimulated by direct electric current in experiments with a frog. Budding young biologists have dissected frogs in classrooms for centuries; frog and toad larvae are studied in endocrinology courses; and many cloning experiments rely heavily on frog embryos. In the 1940s, African clawed frogs were found to be reliable indicators of human pregnancy when injected with the urine of pregnant women; later, the leopard frog replaced the African clawed frog, and eventually any adult male frog was found suitable.

Frogs have made other astonishing contributions to medical science as well. In China, the adrenaline in dried toad skins has been used for centuries to increase patients' low blood pressure. Dart-

Be kind and tender to the Frog,
And do not call him names,
As 'Slimy skin' or 'Polly-wog,'
Or likewise 'Ugly James,'
Or 'Gap-a-grin,' or
'Toad-gone-wrong,'
Or 'Bill Bandy-knees':
The Frog is justly sensitive
To epithets like these.
No animal will more repay
A treatment kind and fair;
At least so lonely people say
Who keep a frog (and by the way,
They are extremely rare).
—Hilaire Belloc,
"The Frog"

A frog found preserved in amber in the Dominican Republic is believed to be 30 million to 40 million years old.

Sometimes when [a frog] begins to feel the chill of autumn, it enters human abodes where it has been known to hop onto a man's lap or abdomen. Some people say that if the tongue of a croaking aquatic frog is placed on the head of a sleeper, he will talk in his sleep and reveal secrets.
—Albert the Great,
Man and the Beasts,
1193-1280

White's tree frog

The Indonesian White's tree frog, like its counterparts in Australia, New Guinea, and New Zealand, is a tame and trusting tree frog that often enters homes in search of food. The unusually smooth skin of the White's tree frog secretes chemicals that kill bacteria and viruses and may help to lower high blood pressure.

poison frogs of Central and South America have fascinated Europeans ever since native hunters were first observed applying their dried toxins to arrows and darts. These toxins, German herpetologist Ralf Heselhaus explains in his book *Poison-Arrow Frogs*, "are not used merely for the purpose of frightening off predators. They also prevent bacteria and fungi from colonizing on the frog's permanently moist skin, where they would find ideal conditions for multiplying." Alkaloids present in the skin secretions of dart-poison frogs became the subject of extensive pharmacological investigation by the National Institute of Arthritis, Metabolism, and Digestive Diseases in the 1960s, and some of these alkaloids, called batrachotoxins, may prove highly significant as anesthetics, muscle relaxants, and heart stimulants, toxicologists Charles W. Myers and John W. Daly report.

Peptides secreted by Australian tree frogs kill bacteria and provide a defense against viral cold sores, and serotonin—a hormonelike substance found in secretions from the cane toad—is known to cause blood vessels to contract, thus offering a possible weapon in the fight against heart disease, mental illness, certain cancers, and allergies. Before the Australian gastric brooding frog disappeared altogether, scientists had hoped to determine whether the frog's ability to shut down production of stomach acids (while the female incubated eggs in her stomach) might have useful application to treatment of humans with gastric ulcers.

Recently, research by Dr. Michael A. Zasloff at the National Institutes of Health has led to the discovery of an infection-fighting peptide in the skin of African clawed frogs which he named "magainin." Zasloff has developed two promising drugs, according to medical reporter Betsy Wagner, the first of which, "expected to hit pharmacies in 1996, is designed to fight diabetic ulcers and impetigo, a complex skin disease." Zasloff's second drug targets eye infections, and evidence may yet be found that peptides can fight cystic fibrosis and cancer. Wagner says secretions harvested from frogs also "hold promise as insect repellants, plaque-fighting toothpaste additives, and nontoxic glues." She concludes: "Not since the fabled frog turned into a prince has an amphibian held so much promise."

The application of frogs to human advantage seems practically limitless. In Europe, violinists have rubbed the skin of toads to prevent their fingers from perspiring; in Germany, European tree frogs (*Hyla arborea*) have been kept in glass jars with tiny ladders as indoor weather forecasters. ("On days when the weather will be bad, the frog stays in the water and croaks, but as he senses clearing weather, he ascends part way up the ladder, and, during ultra-fine weather, he is said to be found most often at the top of the ladder," weather expert Albert Lee reports.) In Calaveras County and South Africa, as well as at fairs and festivals all over the world, frogophiles stage frog-jumping contests. Zoos and aquariums report enormous public interest in reptile and amphibian exhibits, and snakes, lizards, and frogs have become increasingly popular in recent years among pet hobbyists. Herpetologists even have their own on-line network, accessible via computer modem.

Clearly, there is something about frogs that inspires a sense of awe, fascination, or tranquillity. As the narrator of T. Coraghessan Boyle's riotous short story "Hopes Rise" declares, after awakening to the news that frog populations around the world are in decline, "Suddenly I was nostalgic: What kind of world would it be without them?"

"I was seized with a desire to know them," the narrator confesses, "touch them, observe their gouty limbs and clumsy rituals, partake once more of the seething life of pond, puddle, and ditch." In short, to celebrate their existence. As Kermit the Frog remarks in *One Frog Can Make a Difference*, "If you wait until the frogs and toads have croaked their last to take some action, you've missed the point."

Can you ever be sure that you have heard the very first wood frog in the township croak? Ah! how weather-wise must he be! There is no guessing at the weather with him. He makes the weather in his degree; he encourages it to be mild. . . . Long before the frost is quite out, he feels the influence of the spring rains and the warmer days. His is the very voice of the weather. He rises and falls like quicksilver in the thermometer.
—Henry David Thoreau,
Journal, March 24,
1859

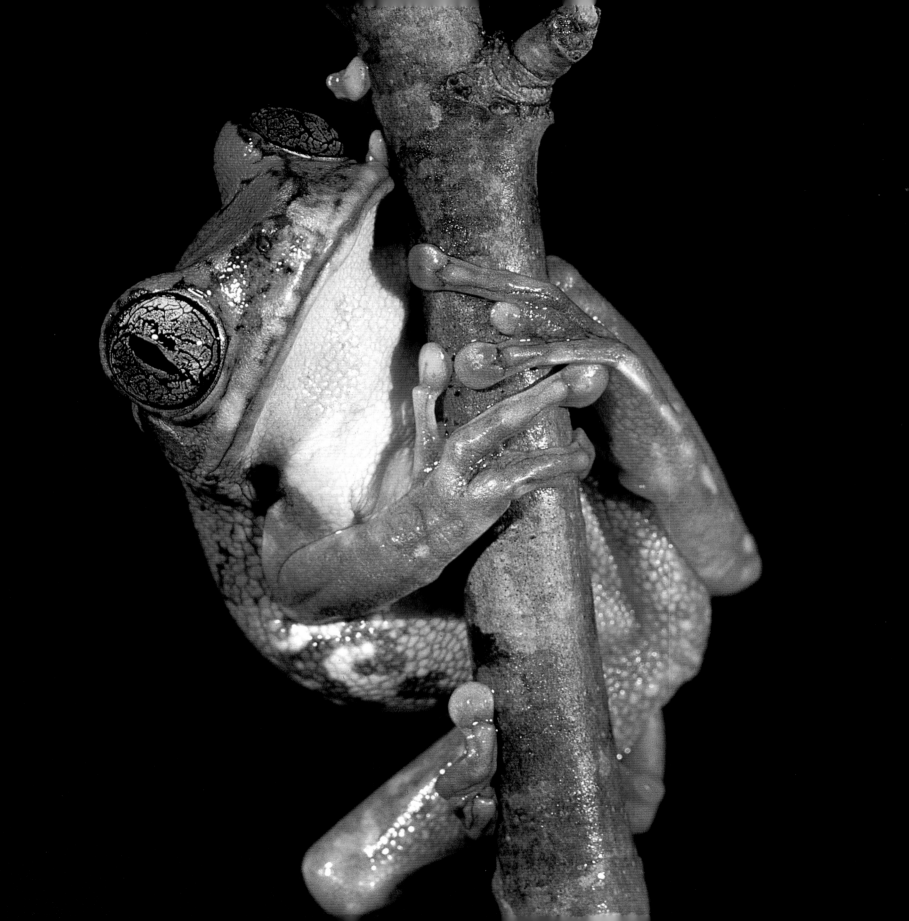

Physical Characteristics and Behavior

THE SKIN OF FROGS AND TOADS IS OFTEN THE FIRST FEATURE TO CLAIM ONE'S ATTENTION. ALTHOUGH the texture itself is of some initial interest, it is the brilliant colors and ornate patterns that bedazzle and beguile.

Contrary to some opinion, not all frogs are green, and not all toads are brown or gray. In fact, William Duellman points out, the array of colors just among Central and South American tree frogs "encompasses the entire visible spectrum." The red-eyed tree frog, for example, has a vivid green head, back, and limbs; bright orange toepads and thighs; and bright blue (or purple) and yellow or cream "flash colors" on its sides. Dart-poison frogs, also from Central and South America, are adorned in spectacular shades of red, blue, green, yellow, orange, gold, bronze, brown, gray, and black—some in eye-catching solids, others in contrasting stripes, bands, spots, speckles, or blotches.

These colors and markings, produced by skin pigments, enhance a frog's chances of survival—blending in with the natural surroundings or gaudily advertising the presence of toxins. The colors can change, however, as pigments move within the cells, producing "chameleonic" effects such as the gray tree frog's transformation from green to gray to brown or black, and the squirrel tree frog's swift change from spotted to unspotted and from chocolate-brown to olive or yellow-green.

Although the skin of a frog generally appears smooth, while that of a toad looks bumpy or warty, this isn't always the case: Many frogs (Argentine horned frogs and gray tree frogs, for example) have rough or highly granular skin (hence the nickname "tree

The frog's life is most jolly, my lads; he has no care Who shall fill up his cup; for he has drink enough to spare.
—Theocritus, Idylls

African big-eyed tree frog
The African big-eyed tree frog, or raucous tree frog, has bulging eyes and prominent disks on its fingers and toes. The male's piercing yack, yack *call can be heard even during cold spells in the winter, echoing from swamps and riverbanks in the Natal region of the Republic of South Africa.*

Golden mantella
The vividly colored skin of Madagascar's golden mantella suggests a warning to enemies that this frog is poisonous, like its relatives the dart-poison frogs. The protective coloration is probably a ruse, however; by mimicking their poisonous kin, golden mantellas may intimidate prospective predators.

toads"), while some toads (e.g., the Colorado River toad) have leathery or relatively smooth skin. This integument serves as the first line of defense, but it plays other strategic roles as well—as a temperature regulator, a respirator, an organ for water absorption, and the site of glands that secrete mucous and poisons.

To many observers, a frog's skin seems to change color because the frog has moved to a different background—settling on a green leaf, perhaps, or on the dark-brown bark of a tree. But this notion, H. Rucker Smyth points out, isn't accurate.

"An amphibian's ability to change color is primarily an internal-temperature regulator," he explains. "On a hot dry day, an amphibian will be lighter in color than on a cool wet day. Light colors reflect more of the sun's rays, whereas dark ones absorb most of them." In short, the color changes "to suit the temperature and humidity of his immediate surroundings." (One African tree frog, *Chiromantis xerampelina*, can even turn white to minimize the effects of extreme heat and sunshine.) Other factors besides temperature, humidity, and light contribute to color change, including diet, mood, season, and the texture of the surface on which the frog is perched.

When the temperature drops, a frog can manipulate its body temperature by moving into the sun or onto a warm surface (such as a road); when the temperature goes up, the frog can cool off by moving into the shade or tucking its arms and legs under its body to reduce the amount of skin exposed to the heat.

Another method of coping with extreme heat is to lubricate the skin. Secretions from mucous glands, located all over the body, keep the skin moist and retard evaporation; among aquatic species, these secretions also reduce friction in water. Specialized mucous glands also produce sticky secretions on the thumbs and chests of some males to facilitate amplexus, and others exude a gluelike substance on the adhesive disks of tree frogs. In South America, several species of tree frog even coat their bodies with a waxy secretion to inhibit water loss.

All frogs and toads require water to provide their bodies with essential liquids, but they do not obtain it by drinking. (Actually, one species of South American tree frog, *Phyllomedusa sauvagei*, may "drink" by letting drops of water roll into its mouth.) Since the skin of all amphibians is permeable, frogs and toads are able to absorb their water cutaneously. Observers have noticed that frogs and toads soak up a good deal of moisture through the skin on their hind legs. After confinement for several days in a dry location, for example, Southern and Woodhouse's toads will hop "eagerly" to water and squat contentedly in the shallows, Dickerson reports. From time to time, they may also lift their wet hind feet and rub water across their back and sides, or apply it to their eyes and head with their hands.

During periods of drought, many species retreat underground and estivate in a torpid state until conditions improve; some, such as the African bullfrog and several South American and Australian species, encase their bodies in a cocoon-like parchment to resist moisture loss.

The mucous secretions that keep the skin of a frog moist also provide a convenient surface for "passive" exchange of gases. Lacking ribs, frogs rely on cutaneous respiration to supplement oxygen intake by the lungs and buccal cavity (or gills in tadpoles).

In addition to mucous, frogs and toads possess at least some trace of poison, although the concentrations and potency vary considerably. In particular, the parotoid glands of toads, located just behind the eyes, secrete toxins that act as a powerful deterrent against enemies.

The toad is a "moveable drugstore," authority Robert DeGraaf declares. Scientists regard the toad as a "veritable chemical factory," he writes, "containing hallucinogens, powerful anesthetics and chemicals that affect the heart and nervous system." If a toad is taken into an animal's mouth, adrenal hormone-like substances in its secretions are quickly absorbed by membranes in the mouth and throat, paralyzing the respiratory system and overstimulating the heart rate, causing a lethal heart flutter. If digested and absorbed into the victim's bloodstream, however, other chemically active components trigger a reaction that slows down the heartbeat, causing heart failure and death.

The psychoactive agents in toad venom are well known among "toad smokers" (persons who smoke dried venom) and "toad lickers"; the hallucinogenic highs described by experimenters range from a slight buzz to "a rocket trip into the void." Consumption of halluci-

Dart-poison frog
The yellow-and-black color morph of Dendrobates leucomelas, *a dart-poison frog from Venezuela's lowland rain forests, is one of several color variations associated with this species. While the bright hues of these daytime-active frogs warn off most enemies, they also attract the attention of Native Americans, who dip arrowheads and darts in the frogs' poisonous skin secretions.*

The African tree frog can turn white to combat the effects of extreme heat and sunshine.

nogenic alkaloids in the secretions of toads dates back hundreds, if not thousands, of years, and physicians and healers in all corners of the world have long ascribed medicinal value to powdered toad, toad ashes, toad pellets, toad grease, and tincture of toad when treating toothache, dropsy, rheumatic pains, bubonic plague, epilepsy, tumors, and cancer.

Frogs produce poisons too, but they are usually less potent than the toxins of toads. Humans who handle frogs should avoid rubbing their eyes or touching their lips, since the secretions can irritate or sting (collectors who pick up African red-banded crevice creepers or certain West Indian tree frogs sometimes find their

hands breaking out in a rash).

By far the most toxic families of frogs are the brightly colored dart-poison frogs of Central and South America, whose skin secretions have been used for centuries by hunters who rub the poisons on the tips of their arrows or blow-pipe darts. Secretions from the yellow-and-black *Dendrobates tinctorius*, for example, are especially potent—attacking the nervous system in much the same way as the venom of cobras and coral snakes. According to Charles W. Myers and John W. Daly, who have studied dart-poison frogs for more than twenty years, just holding this particular species in your hand can be dangerous. A single specimen of another species they have described, *Phyllobates terribilis*, can produce enough toxins to kill an estimated twenty thousand laboratory mice—or up to ten humans.

"Scientists have identified many of the toxins that give poison-dart frog skin its lethal quality," Kathryn Phillips reports. "However, researchers are still stumped where the skin gets the toxins in the first place." Some scientists, she says, "speculate that something specific to the frogs' natural home—perhaps in the diet of wild insects—provides the toxins." According to Roger Prince, dart-poison frogs may have "an ability to culture toxin-producing bacteria on their skins, and the presence or absence of such bacteria would explain the range of toxicities."

From time to time, all frogs and toads must shed their skins—some more frequently than others. While the scaly, paper-thin skins shed by snakes and lizards provide tangible evidence of reptile moltings, skins shed by amphibians aren't left lying around for humans to discover—instead, most are eaten. (Some aquatic species, however, let their skins float away.) Whether it is an adult toad that

Gray tree frog
The rough, granular skin and variable colors of the gray tree frog provide excellent camouflage when it perches on the lichen-covered bark of trees.

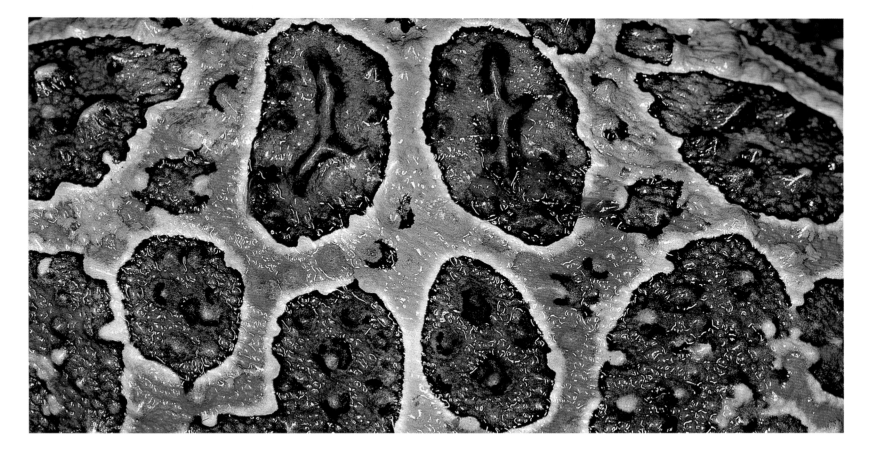

Top: Argentine horned frog
The Argentine horned frog has rough, highly granular skin, hence the nickname "tree toad."

Left: Asian leaf frog
Cryptic coloring and fleshy "horns" over the eyes and snout of the fierce-looking Asian leaf frog, or Asiatic horned frog, provide camouflage when it buries itself in dried leaves on the forest floor in Thailand, Malaysia, Indonesia, and the Philippines.

molts several times a year, or a green tree frog that sheds nearly every day, the animal usually accomplishes its task in a matter of minutes. The process generally begins with yawning motions, to stretch and loosen the skin, and humping of the back, which encourages the skin to split. By rubbing its body with its hind legs and front feet and pulling the skin into its mouth, the frog deftly rids itself of its old skin and reveals a gleaming new skin underneath.

Top: Chinese microhylid
Intricate marbled patterns on the back and legs of the Chinese microhylid make this frog difficult to see among the leaves of Asian forests. Swirling patterns on amphibians and reptiles often inspire cultures to imitate nature in their art.

Right: Southern toad
A Southern toad rests among the dry leaves of a live oak tree. These toads hide by day and hunt at night, emerging from beneath rocks and logs or burrows in suburban gardens to catch insects attracted to outdoor lights.

Vision

When the witches in Shakespeare's *Macbeth* ordered up "eye of newt, and toe of frog," they must have gotten their body parts mixed up—it is the *eyes* of frogs and toads that are magical in appearance. In fact, the color of the iris, the shape of the pupil, and the bulging eyeballs are often a frog's most striking features.

The eyes of frogs and toads come in a spectacular range of colors, from the metallic gold, silver, bronze, and copper hues (sometimes latticed with flecks of black) of many toads and "true frogs" to the vivid red, orange, yellow, blue, and creamy-white tones of tropical tree frogs. Not all

irides (irises) are colorful, however; some are dull brown or black, while others pick up patterns or stripes from the face to help the eye blend in with the head.

"They are undoubtedly the most beautiful eyes in the Animal Kingdom," declares H. Rucker Smyth. "If you look at the gold-flecked eyes of a toad, you will agree with Shakespeare that he 'wears yet a precious jewel in his head,' lovelier by far than any diamond ever could be."

Just as the colors of the irides vary, so too do the shapes of the pupils. In most frogs and toads, the pupil is horizontal, expanding in size to compensate for diminished light and contracting to shut

Red-eyed tree frog
In close-up, the iris of the red-eyed tree frog is a spectacular red or vermilion, with a dark vertical pupil similar to that of a cat. This pupil dilates at night when the tree frog is active, expanding to enhance the frog's vision.

African big-eyed tree frog
The bulging eyes of the African big-eyed tree frog are a striking copper and bronze color, set against formidable cat-like pupils.

Green tree frog
Green tree frogs and other species are apparently farsighted, able to see their prey better at a distance than right under their nose. Green tree frogs swallow insects like this katydid whole; at night, after ingesting a lightning bug, a green tree frog will light up dramatically.

out strong sunlight. Nearly all frogs and toads native to the United States have horizontal pupils, including "true frogs" such as bullfrogs, leopard frogs, and wood frogs; tree frogs and their allies; and "true toads" such as the American, Southern, Colorado River, and Fowler's toad.

Vertical pupils, however, are found in the spadefoot toads of North America (also Europe, Asia, and Africa); the tailed frog of the Pacific Northwest; many tree frogs of Central and South America, including the red-eyed tree frog; and the midwife toad of Europe.

A few less-common shapes are apparent, too, including pupils that are round (in tomato frogs, African clawed frogs, Surinam toads, and narrow-mouthed toads); triangular or heart-shaped (in fire-bellied toads); hourglass-shaped (the African sand toad); and diamond-shaped (the Asiatic horned frog and Bruno's bony-headed frog of Brazil).

The prominent, nearly spherical eyeballs mounted on top of or on opposite sides of the head provide a remarkable field of vision, only about 40 percent of which is truly "binocular"—i.e., viewed by both eyes simultaneously. Instead, each eye commands its own field of vision, not only in front of the frog, but also to the side and partially to the rear. The size of the eyeballs varies a bit from species to species, but, in general, they are larger in tree-dwelling and terrestrial species and smaller in aquatic and burrowing species. The upper and lower eyelids are thick layers of skin that offer the eyeballs some protection; in addition, a nearly transparent nictitating membrane can be drawn up to protect the rest of the eye, especially when swimming.

Curiously, these eyeballs do more than just provide the frog with sight—they also can be lowered into the roof of the

mouth to help the frog swallow large articles of food. (The added pressure assists the teeth in forcing food into the gullet.)

Even though a frog's keen vision is its chief means of locating food, most frogs and other amphibians are actually far-sighted. What that means is, while they can see objects quite well at a distance (up to about 40–50 feet or 12–15 meters), they cannot see things well that are directly beneath their nose. Frogs probably detect small objects best at a distance of a few feet, Dickerson reports; toads, on the other hand, are "less far-sighted" than

Southern leopard frog
The Southern leopard frog is active primarily at night but may also be found during daylight hours in meadows or in water near the banks of streams, ponds, and lakes. With only its eyes protruding from the duckweed, this spotted frog blends in well with its surroundings.

frogs. In their natural habitat, frogs that have congregated in choruses will abruptly stop singing when they see an intruder (or his shadow) approaching; noises made by an unseen intruder, however, are less likely to have the same effect.

It is well known, especially among zoo collectors and hunters who "gig" frogs in the South, that the eyes of frogs and toads (as well as alligators and lizards) will reflect a beam of light from a flashlight at night. This reflection—a sure giveaway to the frog's whereabouts—is caused by a concave mirror-like device that is present in the eyes of many twilight-active and nocturnal species. Amphibians are also attracted to light—street lights, porch lights, billboard lights, interior house lights—because these lights attract their favorite food: insects.

Not much is known about amphibians' ability to see colors, although one scientist suggested as early as 1910 that certain frogs show a "marked preference" for green or blue light. In the early 1960s, W.R.A. Muntz conducted a series of laboratory experiments in which frogs not only demonstrated they could distinguish the color blue but also indicated a preference for blue light over other colors and darkness.

"I think it is quite possible," Muntz concluded, "that the function of the blue-sensitive system is to direct the jump of the frightened frog in such a way that it will leap into the water to avoid its predators."

*M*ost frogs are far-sighted; they can see objects quite well at a distance up to 40–50 feet (12–15 meters), but they cannot see things well that are directly beneath their noses.

*Sweet are the uses of adversity,
Which, like the toad, ugly
and venomous,
Wears yet a precious jewel in his head.
—Shakespeare, As You Like It,
1599–1600*

Glass large-eyed frog
The glass large-eyed frog of Ethiopia, Rwanda, and Burundi is active by night, when it jumps from stem to stem in search of insect prey. Its large, sticky toepads provide a firm grip on reeds and leafy vegetation.

Taste

"While the frog is a gourmand, he is nothing of an epicure," Samuel Holmes observed many years ago in his classic text on frogs. "Almost any sort of living creature is acceptable to him."

Most frogs and toads are indeed indiscriminate feeders. (Some observers joke that frogs see everything that moves in one of three lights: If it's smaller than they are, it's a prospective meal; if it's their own size, it's a prospective mate; if it's larger than they are, it's probably an enemy.) Accordingly, biologist G. K. Noble asserts, most adult amphibians "seem to have little need of a well-defined sense of taste."

Dickerson agrees that the sense of taste in frogs is present only to a "small degree," but others aren't so sure. Mertens, for example, claims that a "true sense of taste is very delicate in most amphibians and reptiles." In any event, taste buds are found in cells distributed throughout much of the interior of the mouth, including the tongue, jaws, and palate, and experiments suggest they are highly sensitive to salty, acidic, and bitter flavors.

Certainly anyone who has watched a frog sample a variety of insects over time has probably seen the frog spit out more than one objectionable bug. Stag beetles are frequently rejected because of their sharp pinching mandibles; other insects secrete chemicals that leave a bad taste in the frog's mouth. Sometimes a frog not only ejects an offensive insect from its mouth, it also flicks it away dismissively with its hands.

Frogs and toads are equipped with remarkable tongues. Long and sticky, these muscular organs can flip food into the frog's mouth faster than the human eye can see. Tongues come in two varieties: Most are attached at the front of the mouth and have a tip shaped like a capital "M"; others are attached to the floor of the mouth. The African clawed frog and the Surinam toad lack tongues altogether, but both aquatic species can suck particles of food directly into their mouths (along with water, which is then forced out), and they also use their long, pointy fingers to maneuver food into their mouths.

Most frogs have tiny teeth positioned on their upper and lower jaws or on the roof of the mouth (or, in the case of toads, on the lower jaw only). These teeth aren't for chewing, but rather for subduing prey, swallowed live and whole, and preventing it from backing out of the mouth.

rogs and toads have remarkable tongues that are long, sticky, and muscular, allowing them to flip food into their mouth faster than the human eye can see.

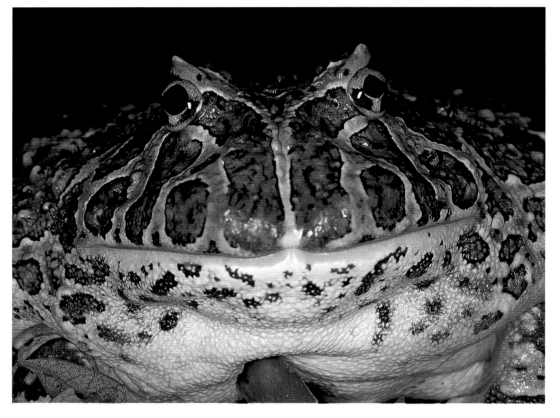

Argentine horned frog
The Argentine horned frog has an enormous mouth and an appetite to match. Equipped with sharp teeth, it smacks its jaws shut with an audible snap and will not hesitate to advance on a larger adversary or a human.

Smell

While a sense of smell is important to most animals for food recognition, it apparently plays a less significant role in most frogs and toads, zoologists have concluded. There are exceptions, however, including aquatic species such as the African clawed frog and species that burrow in the ground or live in caverns.

Chemical receptors are located in the nostrils and Jacobson's organ, the latter a mechanism found in many amphibians and reptiles that tests the contents of the mouth and allows for ejection of undesirable articles. A frog's nostrils are usually visible near the tip of its snout, although the length of the snout itself can vary considerably, from the pug nose of the turtle frog (*Myobatrachus gouldii*) of Western Australia and the flat-faced frog (*Breviceps mossambicus*) of Africa to the triangular snout of Darwin's frog (*Rhinoderma darwini*) and the protruding beak of the spatulate-nosed tree frog (*Triprion spatulatus*) and South American casque-headed frog (*Trachycephalus jordanii*).

The strong odors of algae and other decaying pond matter are believed to send chemical signals that guide certain frogs back to the ponds where they were born. Experiments involving leopard frogs, cane toads, and the Western toad (*Bufo boreas*) have demonstrated that "these species are capable of locating prey by olfactory cues alone," Duellman and Trueb report. The role of olfaction in prey detection among other species of frogs and toads is probably "much more common" than studies indicate, they add.

Casque-headed tree frog
The length and shape of a frog's snout vary considerably from species to species. The elongated snout of this South American casque-headed tree frog is useful for pushing aside leaves and branches, permitting this nocturnal frog to tuck itself into tight hiding places during the day.

37

Sounds seem to reinforce a frog's awareness and body preparedness, but a visual stimulus is required before their motor response kicks in.

Pig frog
A frog's tympanic membrane, or external "eardrum," can be seen behind and slightly below the eye. This pig frog of the lower southeastern United States joins other males in loud midnight choruses that echo through the swamps, resembling the grunts of pigs or the bellows of alligators.

Hearing

The grand performances of frog choruses would be of little avail if frogs themselves could not hear. Although their range of sound perception is not as well developed as that in humans, their sense of hearing is still quite keen. Most frogs and many toads have a prominent round or oval external membrane called the tympanum, located behind and slightly below the eye. Corresponding to the internal tympanum or eardrum of many vertebrates, this relatively large membrane receives sound waves and transmits the vibrations to the middle and inner ear.

The size of and distance between a frog's external "eardrums" apparently correlate with the frequency and wavelength of the male's call. One way to tell certain male and female frogs apart (bullfrogs, for example) is to compare the size of the tympanum to that of the eye—in males, the tympanum is larger; in females, the ear and eye are approximately the same size.

The tympanic membrane absorbs sound whether the frog is on land or underwater; in fact, Dickerson says, hearing may actually be keenest when the eardrum is half exposed to the air and half submerged in water.

For frogs, "sounds seem mostly to reinforce visual awareness and body preparedness," Smyth notes. "A sudden loud noise will startle a human being into action, but the same noise merely puts the amphibian on guard and ready to flee. It seems to require vision fully to interpret the sounds it hears." Laboratory experiments indeed suggest that frogs require a visual stimulus before their motor response kicks in.

Red-eyed tree frog

Vocalizations

"Perhaps the reason frog songs are not generally appreciated," Florida naturalist Archie Carr once observed, "is that they are sung in places where mosquitoes and snakes live."

Exactly so. Frog choruses generally croon in the vicinity of water—prospective breeding grounds to which the musically inclined males hope to lure willing females. But these same swamps and wetlands, lakes and ponds also attract insects and other creatures that send humans packing; as a result, many stirring serenades go unheard.

Furthermore, these vocalizations usually commence after sundown, when Americans whose forebears once sought relief outdoors on their front steps or porches now retreat to air-conditioned sanctums and switch on TVs, PCs, and audio systems that drown out the music of the night.

Today, most Americans have probably heard frog songs only as sound effects in motion pictures, where zoological accuracy and fidelity are seldom a concern. In fact, Carr reveals, "ever since the days of the first talking pictures, Hollywood movie-makers have used recordings of the voice of the Pacific tree frog as background sound for scenes anywhere from New Guinea to the Carolinas." The Pacific tree frog, it turns out, is the only American species that produces the celebrated *ribbit* sound.

During the eighteenth and nineteenth centuries, visitors to America often marveled at the "frog music" they encountered on these shores. One British tourist wrote: "To the stranger walking for the first time in these woods during the summer, this appears the land of enchantment; he hears a thousand noises, without being able to discern from whence or from what animal they proceed, but which are, in fact, the discordant notes of five different species of frogs!"

Another Englishman gushed that "the first frog *concert* I heard in America was so much beyond anything I could conceive of the powers of these musicians that I was truly astonished, in a large swamp, where there were at least ten thousand performers—and not two *exactly* in the same pitch."

Since relatively few tourists or natives nowadays traipse into marshes and backwoods at night (or during rain showers), the voices of frog musicians have had to be brought out of the humid swamplands for more universal appreciation. Over the past few decades, advances in portable cassette recorders and microphones have

Frogs do for the night what birds do for the day: they give it a voice. And the voice is a varied and stirring one that ought to be better known.
—Archie Carr,
The Everglades, 1973

Green frog
The green frog, a resident of the eastern United States, utters a piercing yelp when startled, often just before leaping to safety in nearby water. The tympanum of the male green frog is generally larger than the eye, while the female's is roughly the same size or smaller.

Bullfrog

The bullfrog, one of North America's largest frogs, is famous for its deep bass jug-o'-rum, jug-o'-rum *call, which reminds some listeners of a bull. Males establish and defend their own territories, sitting in the water for hours at a time with only their heads exposed, waiting for prey or prospective mates.*

enabled researchers to tape the songs of frogs and toads in their native habitats and study the recordings in studios with sound analyzers, which can isolate distinct characteristics of calls and facilitate identification of species.

Anyone who has ever listened to one of these recordings (available at many bookshops, nature and wild-bird stores, and libraries), or who has gone out at night to eavesdrop on what John Muir called "the love-songs of the frogs," has likely discovered a whole new universe of sounds, some of which rival the music of birds in their richness and beauty.

As the first land animals with vocal cords, frogs "probably fathered all of the vertebrate music on earth," nature writer Edward Hoagland once reflected. Today, more than 150 million years later, each

species of frog has evolved its own distinct calls, encompassing an extraordinary range of pitches, tonal qualities, and rhythms. As one visitor to Philadelphia put it nearly two hundred years ago: "The *treble* is performed by the tree frogs; the next in size are our *counter tenors*; a still larger species sing *tenor*; and the *under part* is supported by the bullfrogs, which bellow out the bass."

Just why frogs and toads came to produce these sounds—as do insects, birds, and bats—may be explained by Duellman and Trueb's observation that sound production is common "in animals that jump or fly, leaving no continuous trail to be followed by chemosensory means."

Of course, frogs and toads communicate in other ways too, but their musical repertoires (some melodious, others grat-

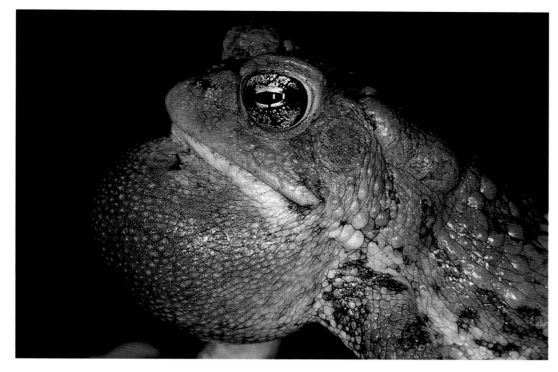

American toad
The vocal sac of the American toad vibrates rhythmically when the male serenades the opposite sex with his sweet, high-pitched trill. At the turn of the century, one herpetologist observed that this toad's song sounds like the opening movement of Beethoven's "Moonlight Sonata."

ing), sound amplification, and chorus structures are unquestionably among their most engaging features. Categorized by function, the calls in a frog's repertoire perform at least half a dozen different roles.

The best-known of the recognized vocalizations is the advertisement call—also known as the breeding call or mating call—performed by males, often in concert with other males, during the breeding season. This season extends from early spring through late summer in the United States (though sometimes longer in warmer regions), or during the rainy season in countries with varying climatic conditions. The advertisement call announces the existence and whereabouts of sexually mature frogs—presumably to attract receptive females of the same spe-

cies, or to direct other males to the breeding site to assemble choruses, or to alert rival males of the same (or different) species that the breeding territory is already occupied.

Humidity, precipitation, temperature, and hours of daylight can all influence breeding behavior and thus affect the advertisement call, while the size of the frog can also have an impact on vocalizations. Ordinarily, the smaller the frog, the higher the frequency or musical pitch of its call; the larger the frog, the lower its frequency and often the longer the duration of the call. When hundreds or thousands of males congregate and sing as a chorus, the "marsh music" they produce can sometimes be heard at distances of half a mile or more.

In North America, many species are

Colorado River toad
The Colorado River toad, or Sonoran Desert toad, has smooth, leathery skin, elongated parotoid glands behind the tympanum, and white warts near the end of the jawline. The male's weak call is said to resemble the sound of a ferryboat whistle.

named for their calls—the pig frog (*Rana grylio*), for example, grunts like barnyard livestock; the carpenter frog (*Rana virgatipes*) sounds like "two carpenters hammering nails slightly out-of-synch," Lang Elliott says; the barking tree frog (*Hyla gratiosa*) yaps like a hound; and the bird-voiced tree frog (*Hyla avivoca*) whistles with a birdlike trill. Countless other species have common names of this sort too, including the sheep frog, bullfrog, cricket frog, squirrel tree frog, chorus frog, chirping frog, and spring peeper.

Scientists are still debating whether female frogs favor certain calls (and, hence, their callers) for their acoustic properties—deeper, longer, or louder calls perhaps signaling older, larger, or healthier males, more fit for propagating the species—although other factors are probably responsible as well. Virtually all males are capable of producing the advertisement call, with the apparent exceptions of the striped mountain toad (*Bufo rosei*) of South Africa, the tailed frog (*Ascaphus truei*) of North America, and a few other stream- and river-dwelling species whose voices would likely be inaudible over the sound of rushing water.

A second recognized type of vocalization is the release call, a sharp chirping sound, accompanied by energetic vibration of the body, made when a male inadvertently clasps another male (or, in some cases, an unreceptive female) during amplexus. The function of this call quite clearly is to "alert the male on top that a mistake has been made," Elliott says, "and encourage him to dismount."

Barking tree frogs
The harsh arrk-arrk-arrk *call of the male barking tree frog reminds Southerners of the barking of hounds.*

The distress call is a scream, wail, or other loud cry emitted by a frog or toad (usually with its mouth wide open) when seized by a predator such as a snake, bird, or mammal. The apparent purpose of the cry is to startle or disorient the predator and thereby effect the release of the victim. In some species, this cry sounds unnervingly like "a cat in distress," Duellman and Trueb report; in bullfrogs, the high-pitched scream is reminiscent of a human voice.

Aggressive calls (or "encounter calls") are sounded by territorial males of some species, usually in anticipation of physical contact. If an approaching male fails to retreat, the resident male may charge, butt, or even wrestle with the intruder in an attempt to evict him from the immediate area. The sounds may vary from a whoop or yelp among gray tree frogs and a "hiccup" in bullfrogs to a chuckle in leopard frogs and a stuttering trill in spring peepers.

The alarm call is a loud, explosive squeak uttered just before some frogs dive into the water for safety. This call of warning, many scientists presume, alerts other frogs to the presence of an intruder or enemy. The green frog (*Rana clamitans*) of North America, for example, invariably issues an explosive, high-pitched cry and leaps into the air when startled by humans, thereby earning the nicknames "screaming frog" and "bawling frog."

Some male tree frogs and other non-aquatic species produce a rain call—a series of hoarse, raspy-sounding notes issued on the approach of a rain shower or in humid weather. This call generally resounds from locations away from the breeding site and may be in response to seasonal hormonal changes.

While the males are responsible for most of the music-making, females of a few species do have recognizable voices (leopard frogs and bullfrogs, for example), and many females will grunt or chirp if provoked. Still, it is the males who converge each spring at the breeding grounds to sing lustily in ear-splitting choruses or perform together in duets or trios. A chorus of spring peepers consists of many such trios, some synchronized in a recognizable rhythm; other species, such as bullfrogs, perform their underwater or terrestrial arias strictly solo.

"Amidst the babel of voices," herpetologist Robert Mertens once wrote, after listening to a frog concert in the tropics, "sounds probably play a vital part in isolating the different species. It is, indeed, the diversity of the voices which makes it possible for sexual partners of the same species to find each other among so many species all active at the same time and place." In spite of this, related species occasionally do interbreed, although the resulting hybrids are, in Mertens' words,

*E*ach species of frog has its own distinct calls, encompassing an extraordinary range of pitches, tonal qualities, and rhythms.

Green tree frog
The vocal sac of a male green tree frog is inflated like a small balloon to produce a noisy nasal quank-quank-quank *advertisement call. Green tree frogs respond not only to one other, but to other stimuli as well; this particular frog was overheard calling at the sound of a washing machine, a popcorn popper, a dog lapping water, a car alarm, cannon fire in a Civil War movie, and Scott Joplin ragtime music.*

Green tree frog

"prejudicial to the continued existence of the species." When hybrid frogs call, their voices are usually intermediate between the two parent species.

Over many decades of collecting and observing frogs, scientists and pet owners alike have noticed that frogs will respond vocally to "nonfrog" stimuli. Some of the more arresting sound sources that have provoked frogs to call are planes, trains, automobiles, fire engines, heavy machinery, sirens, whistles, brush fires, human voices (talking, singing, or imitating frog calls), music (choral or orchestral), and other animals (roosters crowing, dogs barking). My own loquacious green and squirrel tree frogs have sounded off, at all hours of the day and night, in response to the sounds of a washing-machine, a neighbor's car alarm, an outdoor air-conditioning unit, a videotape rewinder, a dog lapping water from a bowl, rhythmic applause on TV shows, and actor Paul Reiser's nervous laughter on "Mad About You."

What makes all these wondrous calls possible—the croaks, clucks, grunts, snores, growls, chirps, trills, whistles, and other sounds—are the resonating vocal sacs (loose pouches of skin) possessed by male frogs. In some species (tree frogs and toads, for example), the inflated chamber resembles a small balloon in the area of the throat when the frog is singing; among other species (such as wood frogs and pickerel frogs), a pair of external sacs that look like large peas are inflated near the shoulders. In yet other species, such as bullfrogs, the throat expands and bulges outward on both sides.

For a frog to sing, it must first inhale air through its nostrils. This air is then pumped back and forth over the vocal cords, which are located on the larynx between the mouth and the lungs. With the mouth firmly closed, the vocal sacs act as resonators, projecting the vibrations and coupling them with the surrounding air "rather like the soundboard of a piano," Halliday and Adler suggest. The flow of air, controlled by muscle contractions or by the larynx, creates a spectrum of calls of varying rates, frequencies, and intensity.

In 405 B.C., the great Greek playwright Aristophanes replicated the sound of a chorus of frogs (probably the European edible frog, *Rana esculenta*) in his satiric comedy *Frogs*—then added his own translation:

> *Brekekekex ko-ax ko-ax . . .*
> All the more
> Shall we chant
> If e'er before
> On a sunlit morn we capered
> Where the flags and rushes tapered,
> Trilling arias ecstatic
> Suited to our sports aquatic,
> Or, in flight from rainy weather,
> Danced in wat'ry regions nether,
> Brightly caroling together
> Many a bubble-and-spray gavotte.

Since Aristophanes' day, countless humans have attempted to describe or recreate the sounds of frogs and toads. The English novelist Leonard Woolf, future husband of Virginia, left readers with a vivid account after a monsoon in Ceylon.

"The ditches were rushing rivers," Woolf wrote; "the ponds were full, the earth was already turning green, the swish of the rain upon the trees was terrific. But deafening, drowning all other noises was the ecstatic chorus of millions of frogs from every ditch and pond and field and compound, a wild, mad, maddening, corybantic, croaking and creaking orgasm of sound of wet, wallowing frogs."

Other Communication

While vocalizations offer the most conspicuous evidence of communication among frogs, they are not the only signals. Other aspects of frog communication include visual displays, chemical cues, release vibrations, and seismic signals.

As herpetologist W. Frank Blair has pointed out, communication among amphibians can be categorized according to functions—that is, as information relating to space, species, sex of the individual, and physiological readiness to mate.

"Most species of frogs are not visually conspicuous," Blair notes, although some, such as the dart-poison frogs of Central and South America and their mimics, are brilliantly colored. The presumed function of the dart-poison frogs' dazzling colors and patterns—combinations of yellow, red, orange, blue, or green, contrasting with dark brown or black—is to warn other animals about highly toxic skin secretions and to discourage them from predation. Of course, this visual-display function requires a learned response from the frogs' enemies, which have to associate the colors with distasteful prior encounters. Certain nontoxic species of frogs whose colors mimic those of poisonous species may have developed their skin colors as a defense mechanism to insure a higher rate of survival.

Dart-poison frogs
The bright colors sported by dart-poison frogs warn predators of toxic skin secretions and may help males defend their territories during courtship. To stimulate a partner, the female blue dart-poison frog (Dendrobates azureus) *nudges the male in the side and strokes his back before the pair retires to a spawning chamber to mate.*

45

Other frogs have evolved "flash colors" on their undersides (e.g., the fire-bellied toad of Europe and Asia), or on their flanks and thighs (the red-eyed tree frog of Central America), presumably to startle or distract would-be predators. Even stranger, perhaps, are the glandular markings on the rear flanks of the Chilean four-eyed frog, which, when exposed, look like two giant eyespots. Other defensive signals include such antipredator postures as mouth gaping by the horned hylid frog (*Hemiphractus fasciatus*), which flaunts a bright orange tongue, and inflating the lungs with air by the European common toad (*Bufo bufo*), which puffs up its body when facing down an enemy.

Another type of color display that may serve as a signal is the brighter pigmentation that appears on the throats of some females during the breeding season. According to William F. Evans, "brilliant yellow and black predominate," with the female throat "more vividly pigmented and usually darker than that of the male."

The so-called "chemical cues" identified among frogs are not those traditionally associated with other animals—i.e., scents that permit reproductive adults to recognize the opposite sex. At present, A. Ross Kiester concludes, "there does not appear to be any evidence that frogs use chemical secretions or pheromones to affect species perceptibility, although this must be the case for at least some species." Instead, biologists suggest, frogs may use chemical cues from algae to locate their original breeding sites year after year. The odors given off by oils in the algae (and perhaps other pond weeds or decaying matter) apparently attract the common European frog (*Rana temporaria*), which may associate the odors with their feeding habits as tadpoles.

Release vibrations, which generally accompany the release call, are a type of signal from one male frog to another in large breeding congresses, where males are in "a high state of sexual excitement" and often attempt to clasp "any object of appropriate size," Blair explains. When a male clasps another in the amplexus position, the vibrations signal for him to cease and desist; sometimes nonreceptive females, including those which have just finished laying their eggs, also vibrate their bodies to discourage clasping males. Some female frogs also signal for a male to release his grip by deflating their lungs, thus reducing the size of their physical girth; if that maneuver fails, they may resort to scraping the male or even kicking him off with their hind legs, Blair reports.

Another recently recognized form of communication is seismic signaling, or thumping, by male white-lipped frogs (*Leptodactylus albilabris*). Experiments conducted by Edwin R. Lewis and Peter M. Narins in Puerto Rico during the 1980s suggest that females of the species are acutely sensitive to these "substrate-borne vibrations" and that males exhibit "conspicuous behavioral responses" to other males that are calling nearby and thumping at the same time.

The Chilean four-eyed frog's glandular markings look like two giant eyespots when exposed.

One hot summer day father told us that we ought to learn to swim. . . . "Go to the frogs," he said, "and they will give you all the lessons you need." —John Muir, The Story of My Boyhood and Youth, 1913

Oriental fire-bellied toad
In its natural habitat, the Oriental fire-bellied toad is well camouflaged from above, but when it wishes to startle an enemy, it arches its back and displays bright orange-red warning colors on the belly and feet, marbled with contrasting black blotches.

Top, bottom, and opposite: Bullfrog
The bullfrog has long, powerfully muscled hind legs for jumping, swimming, and escaping from its many enemies, which include snakes, alligators, otters, hawks, herons, and humans. When leaping off a bank or out of the water, the bullfrog thrusts with its hind legs, often retracting its eyes for protection; the front legs hang in the air before pointing in the direction of its target. These photographs were taken with high-speed strobes with a flash duration of 1/10,000 of a second.

Flying frogs don't actually fly—they glide, sometimes soaring distances of up to 48 feet (14.4 meters) between trees.

Locomotion

Frog-jumping contests such as the annual event in Calaveras County, California, have conditioned many people to think of frogs primarily as "leapers," but these adroit animals move by other means as well. Toads, for example, hop. Arboreal tree frogs climb. Flying frogs glide (or free-fall) with webbed feet serving as makeshift parachutes. Senegal running frogs walk or run. Walking frogs stride slowly. Burrowing toads shuffle and dig. Northern cricket frogs skitter. And all manner of aquatic and terrestrial species swim.

Still, it is the leapers and the climbers, endowed with long hind legs, that amaze observers. When a leopard frog launches itself into the air, or a jittery bullfrog jumps into the water, the powerful extensor muscles in its rear legs perform a remarkable feat.

"Frogs have an inelegant way of taking off from invisible positions on the bank just ahead of your feet, in dire panic, emitting a froggy 'Yike!' and splashing into the water," Annie Dillard wrote in *Pilgrim at Tinker Creek*. But a frog's sudden surprise movements aren't really "inelegant"—rather, they are executed with great dexterity; even the shorter front limbs serve an important function as shock absorbers for the landing.

The size of a frog sometimes fools observers into assuming that the bigger the frog, the longer the leap. Yet the goliath frog of Africa, which exceeds 15 inches (375 mm) from snout to rump, is actually a rather poor jumper, and entrants in the Calaveras County frog-jumping contest have proved embarrassing duds. Well-hyped bullfrogs can excite audiences with their proven ability to leap

*T*he Indian water frog can actually run across the surface of water for distances of up to several yards.

Red-eyed tree frogs
Red-eyed tree frogs are graced with astonishingly long, slender hind legs and large, bright orange toepads on their hands and feet. These nocturnal frogs walk purposefully across leaves or stems when stalking insect prey, occasionally stepping on other frogs, but they can spring explosively when agitated.

nine times the length of their body, but smaller frogs can jump even farther relative to their size. The leopard frog, for example, can leap fifteen times its body length, and the Southern cricket frog (*Acris gryllus gryllus*) can jump an astonishing thirty-six times its body length.

The arboreal climbing species have long hind legs, too, with "suction" disks on the tips of their fingers and toes for adhesion. (Glands on these toepads secrete a sticky mucous that aids in climbing.) Whether clinging to branches and leaves or scaling the smooth glass walls of a terrarium, tree frogs and their relatives demonstrate extraordinary skill in catching insect prey and simply staying aloft in the wind or on a slick surface. Cochran

once referred to tree frogs as the "acrobatic clowns" of the amphibian world, "since they may be seen hanging by one toe from a twig, or pressed flat against a vertical tree trunk, or balanced lightly on a swaying reed beside a river."

Toads, on the other hand, have shorter hind legs, so they generally hop or walk. The European common toad, for example, makes slow "grovelling movements," according to Maurice and Robert Burton, and when this toad joins others of its species to migrate as many as two or three miles to breeding pools, the processions can be quite spectacular. Toad lovers throughout Great Britain will turn out at night to help toads cross highways, since the animals' slow pace otherwise causes many to fall victim to speeding lorries and motorcars. "It's a high-pressure job," *Newsweek* correspondent Nancy Cooper wrote, "particularly after 11 P.M. Says herpetologist Tom Langton: 'That's pub-closing time, and lots of toads get squashed in the rush home.'"

In Malaya, Japan, India, and other Asian countries, some arboreal frogs have developed extensive webbing on their hands and feet that can be spread like parachutes when they jump. These so-called "flying frogs" don't actually fly, of course, they glide—but some can navigate distances of up to 48 feet (14.4 meters) between trees.

The swimmers—such as the bullfrog and the pig frog—also have wide webbing on their hind feet, enabling them to propel themselves through their aquatic environment. Bullfrogs are powerful swimmers, and their hind legs are particularly long, measuring 7–10 inches (175–250 mm). "To see a bullfrog swim," herpetologist H. Rucker Smyth once declared, "is to witness frog swimming at its best."

While many species of frogs and toads can be recognized by their characteristic styles of locomotion—including the methodical walking and energetic running of the African kassina frogs—perhaps none is quite as astonishing as the Indian water frog (*Rana cyanophlyctis*). Like the basilisk lizard and an iguana found in Cuba, this amphibian can actually run across the surface of water for distances of up to several yards. The Northern cricket frog (*Acris crepitans crepitans*) of the American East and Southeast also has been known to "skitter" across water. This frog "literally skips or bounces across the surface of the water in a series of rapid jumps," Halliday and Adler report.

Top: Tree frog
The almost giraffelike reticulated patterns on the back of Hyla vulvosa *help this tree frog blend in with bark and leaves when searching for insects to eat.*

Left: Red-legged running frog
The red-legged running frog of West Africa and coastal East Africa is a nocturnal ground-dweller found primarily in rain forests. Like other running frogs, it rarely hops or jumps, preferring instead to stretch its long legs and run or walk.

American toads
The male American toad performs his advertisement call at night, but once a pair begins mating, they may remain locked in the amplexus position well into the daylight hours. The presence of nearby humans and traffic will not deter their ardor as the female deposits her long strands of eggs in shallow streams and on nearby banks.

Reproduction

When a frog he would a-wooing go, he set off with his opera hat in the time-honored nursery rhyme. But most male frogs, lacking hats, court members of the opposite sex by serenading them with songs, ranging from the tremulous trills of toads and sleigh-bell sounds of spring peepers to the rattling snores of leopard frogs and bellows of bullfrogs. These male advertisement calls, often performed by massive choruses, direct females to the breeding sites—usually permanent or temporary standing water. Most, though by no means all, frogs spawn in water; in fact,

when it comes to their "manner of reproduction," Mattison says, "frogs are the most diverse vertebrates on earth."

Generally speaking, frogs and toads resort to one of two basic reproductive strategies: explosive breeding or prolonged breeding. Explosive breeders, such as spadefoot toads, wood frogs, and leopard frogs, migrate to temporary rain pools or ponds and engage in what Smithsonian researcher Kentwood Wells calls "scramble competition."

"The males apparently cannot discriminate visually between males and females," Wells says, "so the search for mates is a trial-and-error process. Males approach and attempt to clasp practically any moving object." In their frenzy to grab a female, males sometimes mistakenly mount a fellow male (who then shakes his body and squeaks a release call) or even a fish, rock, boot, or other object. Female frogs, however, are nearly always larger than their male counterparts, and when they are carrying eggs their girth (and "resistance to compression," as Noble puts it) helps to distinguish them—along with their silence when embraced.

The sudden appearance of water galvanizes explosive breeders to engage in sexual activity before the pools of water can evaporate, with the entire breeding period lasting only a few days or weeks; the procreation season of prolonged breeders, on the other hand, extends over a period of at least a month or longer (or, in some tropical climates, year-round). Vocal competition, spacing between males, territorial defense, and quality of the egg-laying site may ultimately dictate which males achieve reproductive success.

Prolonged breeders, such as bullfrogs, green frogs, pig frogs, and most tree frogs, attract females to their calling sites with their songs, but they usually wait for the

Woodland slough

A woodland slough provides an ideal breeding site for frogs as they emerge from winter hibernation in the mud or surrounding forest. Spring peepers, chorus frogs, leopard frogs, green frogs, and bullfrogs are attracted to duckweed-covered sloughs like this one.

*A frog he would
a-wooing go.
Heigh-ho! says Rowley.
Whether his mother would let him or no.
. . .*

*Pray, Mister Frog, will you give
us a song?
Heigh ho! says Rowley.
Let it be something that's not very long.
—"A Frog He Would
A-Wooing Go"*

female to initiate physical contact—nudging, rubbing, stroking, circling, or even jumping on the male. Male intruders, on the other hand, are often charged, pushed, butted, kicked, or bitten. Resident male green frogs, for example, patrol the perimeters of their shallow-water territories and growl at interlopers, while dart-poison frogs engage in fierce wrestling bouts, during which they stand on their hind legs like pint-sized gladiators.

The male amphibian's mating embrace, known as amplexus, consists of grasping the female from behind and fertilizing the eggs with sperm. (Since male frogs lack a penis, fertilization is external, except among a few species, such as the Puerto Rican coqui frog and the North American tailed frog, whose tail-like copulatory organ permits internal fertilization.) In most species, the male clasps the female firmly under her armpits or in her groin area. ("'Firmly' is a mild word for this nuptial embrace," Smyth says. "If you catch a mated pair of toads, you will find it almost impossible to separate them.") Some species assume more unusual positions, however, including the puffball-shaped African burrowing frog (*Breviceps adspersus*), which "glues" itself to the posterior of the considerably larger and more rotund female, remaining attached for up to three days. In a number of species, the thumbs of the male swell (hence the name "nuptial pads") to provide a better grip on the female's wet, slippery body.

When the female extrudes her eggs, the male covers them with his sperm; his timing must be good, Floridians Winston

American toads

The female American toad may initiate amplexus by nudging a male and turning her back toward him, encouraging him to embrace her. The male's tight clasp stimulates her to discharge her eggs in long jellylike strands, which the male fertilizes externally before they sink to the bottom of the water.

The tiny *Sminthillus limbatus* of Cuba lays a single egg, whereas the cane toad lays some thirty-five thousand.

Frog eggs
Most North American frogs lay their eggs in large frothy masses in shallow water, where the eggs initially float or are secured to water plants. The rate of development varies from species to species, but depositing eggs in large numbers, sometimes communally, enhances prospects for survival.

American toad tadpoles
After hatching, the tiny black tadpoles of an American toad cluster together in swarms, rushing about frantically when disturbed or when exchanging bubbles of air at the surface. These tadpoles race to develop arms and legs before the heat of the sun evaporates their shallow pools.

Williams and Pete Carmichael point out, "because as soon as the eggs contact the water, the protective jelly in which they are carried swells enormously into a protective mass."

The size of the female's egg clutch varies considerably, from the single egg laid by Cuba's tiny *Sminthillus limbatus* to the cane toad's reported thirty-five thousand. The advantage of large numbers, of course, is enhanced prospects for survival. Frog and toad eggs, generally laid in clusters or in long gelatinous strands, lack a shell, so they have an unusually high mortality rate—as grim as 95 percent in some species. Many of these eggs are devoured by fish, newts, frogs, aquatic insects, leeches, and other carnivorous animals; others freeze when temperatures drop suddenly, or are battered by rain or stranded when water in temporary pools evaporates. Today, more and more frog eggs are falling victim to bacteria, industrial pollution, herbicides, pesticides, acid rain, and ultraviolet radiation that invades the earth's atmosphere through thinning stratospheric ozone.

Although most species of frogs and toads deposit their eggs directly in the water, usually on the surface or attached to submerged vegetation, a surprising number have developed alternative strategies. Foam nesters, such as the African gray tree frog, Japanese and Chinese gliding frogs, and the Mexican white-lipped frog, deposit their eggs in frothy nests suspended over (or floating on) water. Whipped up by frenzied kicking of a fluid secreted by the female, the foam hardens "like a meringue," Halliday and Adler explain; it remains in place, or dissolves gradually, until the tadpoles hatch and fall into the water.

Many other modes of reproduction have been identified as well. Some species lay their eggs on the ground, on rocks, on roots, in mud nests, or in burrows near water; others lay their eggs coiled in leaves, damp moss, or water-filled tree cavities. Some females carry their eggs in a brood pouch (the marsupial frog) or spongy layer of skin (the Surinam toad) on their back; some males carry egg strings on their hind legs (the midwife toad); another male picks up the eggs with his tongue and slides them into his vocal sac (Darwin's frog). Some species remain with their eggs to guard them (glass frogs) or to keep them moist (greenhouse frogs); other parents transport their tadpoles to water-filled bromeliads (dart-poison frogs). And the female gastric brooding frog, now believed to be extinct, would swallow her eggs and carry them in her stomach before spitting out the fully developed froglets.

Each freshly laid egg of a frog is a single cell; after fertilization, it undergoes division, or cleavage, into a number of cells. The yolk provides nutrition as the cells grow around it and absorb it during embryo formation. The rate of development is variable, though often highly dependent upon temperature.

When the larva emerges, it looks quite unlike a frog—seemingly all head, plus a tail. The name "tadpole," in fact, derives from this very perception: *Tad* is a corruption of the word "toad," and *pole* comes from the word "poll," which once meant "head"—as in "poll tax," etymologist John Hunt explains. ("Polliwog" is derived from "poll" and "wog," which meant "wiggle.") Europeans as late as the 1500s classified these creatures into two types: those which were produced from "seeds," and those which emerged from dust after summer showers or fell from the sky.

The globe-shaped body of the tadpole soon develops gills, a mouth, and eyes and, with its muscular tail, becomes free-swimming; in its early stages, however, the hatchling rests by holding onto plants or rocks with a pair of oral suckers while drawing nourishment from its yolk supply. After the suckers disappear, a horny beak and toothlike rows of teeth appear that permit the tadpole to graze on algal slime and other pond matter. Most tad-

Newt preying on frog eggs
The red-spotted newt is particularly fond of frog eggs, swimming in and out of the gelatinous egg masses and ripping them apart before devouring the eggs. Sometimes when the temperature drops, a newt will become trapped in the eggs and freeze.

poles are herbivores, but a few—such as wood frogs, some spadefoot toads, and Argentine bullfrogs—are carnivores (or even cannibals).

The metamorphosis of most frogs and toads is relatively rapid, taking from a few days to a few weeks or months; a few species, however, such as the green frog and the bullfrog, may not change into frog form for one or two years. Over time, the tadpole's external gills disappear and are replaced by internal gills. While the front and hind legs develop simultaneously, the rear legs are the first to become visible. The tail eventually begins to shrink, as it is absorbed from within, and the tadpole may begin rushing to the surface to gasp for air or emerge completely from the water to test its future habitat.

Herpetologists, who generally have more success raising tadpoles than amateurs (most of whom discover too late that chlorinated water, warm or cold temperatures, or bad luck with other factors can quickly decimate a jar of tadpoles), have observed that different species have different behavior patterns. Green frog tadpoles, for example, " 'go crazy' every once in a while," Smyth says. "They will flop every which way, much like a fish on land . . . swim on their bellies, right side up, then suddenly flip over and swim on their backs." And the huge 10-inch (250 mm) tadpoles of the South American paradoxical frog (*Pseudis paradoxis*) invert the pattern of other frogs by actually shrinking during metamorphosis into adults that are only about 3 inches (75 mm) in length.

Curiously, while the sex of a tadpole is inherited at birth, its gender "may be reversed by such environmental conditions as food and, above all, temperature," Smyth says. "High temperatures produce mostly males, while low temperatures produce mostly females." At a so-called neutral temperature, "the sex ratio is approximately equal."

While the eggs of frogs and toads are eagerly devoured by leeches, insects, newts, ducks, and other enemies, the young froglets and toadlets are subject to attack as they embark on their new terrestrial careers. Snakes, wading birds, hawks, owls, turtles, and mammals quickly take their toll—along with man and his ubiquitous automobile.

Frog tadpole eating toad eggs
As frog larvae develop, they eat their own jelly mass before scavenging for dead plant and animal matter. Some frog tadpoles are cannibalistic, dining on their own species; here, tadpoles consume the eggs of an American toad.

Newt stalking tadpoles
Red-spotted newts also prey on tadpoles. Young froglets and toadlets are subject to attack as well from snakes, wading birds, hawks, owls, turtles, and mammals as they embark on their new terrestrial careers.

Tadpole eating gray tree frog eggs
Most tadpoles are herbivores, but a few—such as wood frogs, some spadefoot toads, and Argentine bullfrogs— are carnivores, or even cannibals, such as this frog tadpole making a meal of gray tree frog eggs.

Whenever we awoke last night, we heard the hoarse foghorn bellow of the male bullfrogs. Who would think of describing it as a siren song or a call of enticement? Yet each of the males, yellow-throated now in the breeding season, is in truth singing a raucous lovesong at the water's edge.
—Edwin Way Teale,
A Walk Through
the Year, 1978

Bullfrog tadpole
Bullfrog tadpoles are the largest of any North American species, frequently growing five inches or longer. Unlike most other frogs, bullfrog tadpoles in the North generally "winter over" one or two years before metamorphosing into frogs.

From this bank at this spot in summer I can always see tadpoles, fat-bodied, scraping brown algae from a sort of shallow underwater ledge. Now I couldn't see the ledge under the ice. Most of the tadpoles were now frogs, and the frogs were buried alive in the mud at the bottom of the creek. They went to all that trouble to get out of the water and breathe air, only to hop back in before the first killing frost. The frogs of Tinker Creek are slathered in mud, mud at their eyes and mud at their nostrils; their damp skins absorb a muddy oxygen, and so they pass the dreaming winter.
—Annie Dillard, Pilgrim at Tinker Creek, 1974

Cypress lake
A cypress lake in the Mississippi River flood plain offers a favored breeding site for more than a dozen species of frogs. In the winter, when the lake freezes over, these frogs hibernate in the mud below or bury themselves in the nearby shoreline or forest floor.

Gray tree frog
Gray tree frogs survive the winter cold by manufacturing freeze-resistant glycerol, which sees them through their long hibernation period when more than half of their total body water sometimes turns to ice.

Hibernation and Estivation

Unlike the birds of the air, frogs and toads cannot pull up stakes and seek warmer climes when temperatures drop—instead, they must take refuge underground or underwater during the winter months. Hibernation among amphibians, herpetologist Robert Stebbins explains, is a "prolonged retreat from the surface" to escape from the cold; its corollary, pro-

longed retreat to escape from heat or dryness, is called estivation.

Amphibians are ectotherms—that is, they are cold-blooded animals; like reptiles and fish, their body temperatures vary as surrounding temperatures rise and fall. Amphibians have a greater tolerance for cold than reptiles, however, which explains why frogs and toads are seen at higher altitudes and farther north than their reptilian relations.

In the fall, when temperatures begin to drop, a frog's respiration and circulation gradually slacken, and the animals become "more and more lethargic," Dickerson says, "until they sleep." In the spring, as their bodily functions return to normal, frogs emerge from their hibernation. Toads generally hibernate by burrowing into the ground; frogs usually hibernate in the mud at the bottom of ponds, in springs or streams, or in moist spots under decaying vegetation, logs, roots, rocks, or the like.

"Frogs breathe by means of lungs, and at high temperatures they must come to the surface to breathe at frequent intervals," herpetologist James Oliver says, "but at a temperature of 40 degrees Fahrenheit [4.4 degrees Celsius], they can remain totally submerged for days."

Some species hibernate longer than others. Spring peepers and wood frogs, for example, emerge a month or two before bullfrogs and other species. Since wood frogs also range farther north than any other amphibian (well into the Yukon and Northwest Territories of Canada and the tundra of Alaska), biochemists Kenneth and Janet Storey decided the life processes of these frogs merited closer analysis. What they discovered was that wood frogs (along with spring peepers and striped chorus frogs) accumulate "massive quantities" of glucose, the naturally occurring blood sugar of vertebrates, during "freezing episodes." Gray tree frogs, which appeared to be similarly "freeze-resistant," manufacture glycerol. Thus, at least four common species of North American frogs manufacture their own anti-freeze compounds to "survive days or weeks of freezing with as much as 65 percent of their total body water as ice."

If a frog were to enter a location where the cold temperature remained constant—such as a deep well or cave—"hibernation would continue for years perhaps," Dickerson speculates, "until, still sleeping, the creature died from exhaustion of vital forces." Frogs found frozen in blocks of ice, however, have been known to thaw out and survive for short periods of time, Noble reports.

A frog kept indoors during the winter at room temperatures will not feel the need to hibernate, just as those in warmer regions of the South and West will seldom engage in hibernation activities. But if indoor temperatures are permitted to drop—say, when a window or door is opened—green frogs and other species will immediately dive under moss or other vegetation to escape the cold.

Northern leopard frogs are known to hibernate in groups when cold weather sets in, heading for the bottom of ponds or streams to escape freezing temperatures. Oliver recalls the story of a Wisconsin frog hunter "who got 280 pounds [126 kg] of leopard frogs in four hours without moving, simply by collecting them as they hopped toward their winter pool." And a Minnesota outdoorsman, he adds, once found the sandy bottom of a stream "literally paved with hundreds of closely crowded leopard frogs."

Toads reportedly retreat to their underground burrows earlier than do frogs; when they emerge in the spring they instantly become "social creatures" and seek out members of the opposite sex.

Amphibians that estivate underground during periods of extreme heat or dryness, such as spadefoot toads, various desert-living species in Africa, and the water-holding frog in Australia, essentially shut down their body functions until moisture and lower temperatures cue the animals to return to the surface. In recent experiments with spadefoot toads, Lon McClanahan, Rodolfo Ruibal, and Vaughan Shoemaker discovered that silent moistening of the soil above the toads failed to trigger any response, "whereas sprinkling the soil to imitate rain caused the animals to surface." In fact, they found, the toads emerged at the sound of rain alone, even when sheets of plastic prevented the soil from getting wet.

His Mansion in the Pool
The Frog forsakes
He rises on a Log
And statements makes
—Emily Dickinson

Eastern spadefoot toad
Eastern spadefoot toads retreat underground when temperatures soar, digging backwards into sandy soil with crescent-shaped spades on their hind feet. These toads will estivate for weeks at a time, emerging only to eat or to seek a mate when rains create favorable conditions.

Families and Species

THE "QUEER ASSEMBLY" OF CREATURES THAT LINNAEUS LABELED *AMPHIBIA* IN 1758 INCLUDES THE order Anura (frogs), which is divided into roughly twenty-four families (some herpetologists prefer twenty, others say twenty-five). Each family comprises one or more genera, which, in turn, are divided into species. Amphibian classification and nomenclature remain in flux, however, and "as soon as changes are proposed (published) by one or more herpetologists, they are vigorously opposed by others," Roger Conant and Joseph T. Collins note.

For students of North American herpetology, excellent species classifications are available in Conant and Collins' *A Field Guide to Reptiles and Amphibians of Eastern and Central North America* (third edition) and Robert Stebbins' *A Field Guide to Western Reptiles and Amphibians* (second edition). Helpful taxonomies or guides to international species include *Amphibian Species of the World*, edited by Darrel R. Frost; *Living Amphibians of the World* by Doris Cochran; *The Completely Illustrated Atlas of Reptiles and Amphibians for the Terrarium*, by Fritz Obst, Klaus Richter, and Udo Jacob; and the indispensable *Biology of Amphibians*, by William Duellman and Linda Trueb.

Due to the scientific controversies, taxonomic complexities, and linguistic peculiarities of so many families of frogs and toads, we have elected instead to focus on individual species, providing representative examples of widely recognized as well as unusual and idiosyncratic species. In all, some fourteen different families of frogs (including Hylidae, Bufonidae, Ranidae, Centrolenidae, Pelobatidae, Pipidae, Leptodactylidae, Dendrobatidae, Microhylidae, Discoglossidae, Hyperoliidae, Rhacophoridae, Atelopodidae, Phrynomeridae) are featured in the portfolio that follows.

Red-eyed tree frogs
The red-eyed tree frog sports a rainbowlike array of colors, from bright enamel-red eyes and a green backside to blue- or purple-banded flanks, orange feet, and a creamy-white belly and throat. The intensity of these colors varies from one individual to another, and patterns and hues may differ according to geographic location.

Brekekekex ko-ax ko-ax
Brekekekex ko-ax ko-ax
From marsh and mere
Sound again
Your fair refrain
Deep and clear,
O humid race,
Booming the bass
Cadenza
Ko-ax ko-ax.
—Aristophanes,
The Frogs, 405 B.C.

Red-Eyed Tree Frog
Agalychnis callidryas

Judging from its countless public appearances on the covers of wildlife, travel, and photography magazines, the red-eyed tree frog (*Agalychnis callidryas*) of Central America probably ranks as the world's most popular tree frog. Its celebrity is easy to understand, for it is one of the most spectacularly beautiful of all frogs, clad in rich, exotic colors that almost stagger belief. Yet, for all its flash and dazzle—blood-red eyes, neon-green back, blue-striped flanks, cream-colored underside, and orange toepads—this species is remarkably placid and strikes admirers as a truly reflective, even inquisitive-looking creature.

First identified by the noted herpetologist Edward D. Cope in the early 1860s from specimens procured on surveying expeditions in Central America, the red-eyed tree frog was given a scientific name derived from the Greek words *kallos* (which means "beautiful") and *Dryas* (a tree or wood nymph).

According to hylid authority William Duellman, this arboreal species is found chiefly on the Atlantic slopes and lowlands from central Mexico to northern Honduras, and on the Caribbean slopes and lowlands southward to the Panama Canal Zone. It lives in trees in tropical rain forests—sometimes as high up as 50 feet (15 meters)—descending at dusk during the rainy season to breed in ponds and temporary pools.

The mating behavior of the red-eyed tree frog is somewhat unusual, for the female will carry the male on her back while she walks or climbs to a suitable site to deposit her eggs. Females are attracted to males by their *chock-chock* mating call, repeated at intervals of eight to ten seconds. Duellman once observed a female approach a male vocalizing on a tree limb; "the male continued to call as the female placed a hand on his back," he writes, "and did not take notice of her until after she had crawled over him and proceeded a short distance." During amplexus, males often close their eyes as they clasp their mates.

Females deposit clutches of fifty to one hundred eggs on leaves that overhang ponds or streams so that larvae will fall into the water as they hatch. These tadpoles sink to the bottom for a minute or two, before swimming to the surface. If the hatchlings should accidentally fall onto the ground, however, they can flip themselves with their muscular tails to reach the nearby water.

Red-eyed tree frogs
Red-eyed tree frogs live high in trees in tropical rain forests, descending at dusk during the rainy season to breed in ponds and temporary pools.

The red-eyed tree frog lives high up in trees in tropical rain forests—sometimes as high as 50 feet or 15 meters.

Red-eyed tree frog
The "flash colors" of the red-eyed tree frog are visible on the frog's flanks and delicate legs. Though not exposed when the frog tucks in its limbs to sleep, these bright colors are prominently displayed when the frog jumps, startling or confusing its enemies.

In recent years, the highly photogenic red-eyed tree frog has appeared not only on magazine covers but also on T-shirts, sweatshirts, umbrellas, coffee mugs, shower curtains, jigsaw puzzles, and numerous other items. Its high visibility is due in part to the symbolic role it plays as a representative of tropical rain forests currently under siege and disappearing at the rate of approximately one and a half acres every second. No doubt the frog's gentle nature, arresting catlike pupils, crimson-red eyes, matchstick-thin limbs, and spectrum of other vivid colors have contributed to its long-running engagement as a headliner for environmental causes. One hopes it is not a tragic farewell performance.

Green tree frog
These frogs are expert climbers, often seen at night on window screens in the American South, hunting insects attracted to the light. The adhesive disks on their fingers and toes adhere to rough and smooth surfaces alike; in captivity, green tree frogs sleep vertically, nose pointed upward, clinging to a leaf or to the glass side of a terrarium.

Green Tree Frog
Hyla cinerea

When the wife of a University of Florida herpetologist began keeping a journal in 1949 about the animals she encountered in her Gainesville backyard, she had no idea that green tree frogs (*Hyla cinerea*) would soon become cherished consorts.

"We would see them frequently at night around the pool during dry spells," Olive Goin recalls, "or climbing on the window screens with a curious long-legged stalk in search of the insects that are attracted to the house lights." The frogs also turned up during the day, in plain sight, clinging to the walls of their house. "Apparently they're rather restless sleepers," Goin concluded, as the usually nocturnal creatures would often begin to stir in the afternoon.

This frog that so beguiled Olive and Coly Goin has been hailed as "perhaps the most beautiful tree frog of North America" by herpetologist Mary Dickerson, and its recurring appearances at night on window screens across the South—along with its celebrated voice—make it one of this country's most conspicuous frogs.

Green tree frogs—also commonly referred to as rain frogs, bell frogs, cowbell frogs, Carolina tree frogs, and fried bacon frogs—are a smooth, bright apple-green species notable for quick color changes to dark olive, brown, ashy-gray, or even black. Most sport a prominent ivory or yellow stripe along their upper lip, often extending along the side of the body; some also have small yellow or gold flecks on their backs. Also identified by their prominent bronze or golden eyes, the large suction disks on the tips of their fingers and toes, and their long hind legs, these handsome frogs have been dubbed "weather prophets" because of their inclination to sing just before rain showers.

Although high humidity and stormy weather certainly stimulate males to issue their earthy *quank-quank-quank* call (characterized by some imaginative listeners as a cowbell ringing sound, or *bo babe, bo babe*, or *fried bacon, fried bacon*), there is no limit to the catalysts. A green tree frog I kept indoors one summer, for example, responded with equal relish to the sounds of water cycling in a washing machine, a dog lapping noisily from a water dish, a neighbor's car alarm, metal buttons clacking in a clothes dryer, a vacuum cleaner, and tape recordings of other green tree frogs. (House guests were twice rudely awakened at 4 A.M. by the call of this frog, and it had to be temporarily banished.) Photographer John Netherton reports some of his specimens responded lustily to the rhythmic beat of the rock group

The Eagles.

George Porter, another frog enthusiast, recalls that whenever his wife engaged in animated conversations or read aloud, one particularly loquacious green tree frog "would call loudly as long as she spoke" and even increase its tempo "if my wife raised the pitch of her voice."

While the somewhat harsh sound of the male green tree frog may not be pleasing to everyone, it can instill a tremendous sense of awe when congresses of a hundred or more suddenly erupt into song. The resulting cacophony is "nothing short of mind-boggling," Floridians Pete Carmichael and Winston Williams report, particularly since each individual frog "might be calling at a slightly different pitch." More than 150 years ago, one herpetologist observed of green tree frogs that "there seems in general to be one leader of their orchestra, and when he raises his note, hundreds take it up from all parts of the field, and when he stops, the concert is at an end."

During the day, or after a meal, the green tree frog often strikes a serene pose, pulling up its front legs close to its chest and tucking in its toes like a cat. Often the frog will adhere with its powerful adhesive disks to a vertical surface—a leaf, palmetto frond, wall, or glass of a terrarium—its eyes closed to the narrowest of slits, relying on tiny granules of skin on its underside to provide an additional surface for suction. When the frog stirs from its resting position, it may walk on its long legs or jump in the direction of a moving moth or cricket. If it misses, the frog may hang onto the nearest surface, sometimes by only a toe or two, before righting itself and leaping again. The span of the green tree frog's jump has been measured, astonishingly, at 8–10 feet (2.40–3 meters), although the frog itself is only about 1.25–2.50 inches (31–62 mm) long.

Ranging from the Florida Keys north to Delaware, west to southern Illinois, and down the Mississippi River Valley to Texas, green tree frogs live near swamps or at the margins of ponds and other bodies of water, where they perch on lily pads or cling to the shady undersides of leaves growing on vines, ferns, shrubs, and other vegetation, including wild rice, corn, and okra. Some years ago, in the Everglades, naturalist Archie Carr came across a "gangling, slim-legged" green tree frog in a stand of young red mangroves, "industriously catching mosquitoes."

"You rarely find one hunting in the daytime," he recalled, "but this one was in a perfect frenzy of mosquito-catching. . . . Yet not one of them sat on the naked frog. It seemed totally immune to the hordes, as if shielded from them by some personal secretion of bug repellant. On straw-thin hopping legs it dangled and swung from twig to twig, snapping at the inexhaustible store of prey on the glossy leaves."

During the breeding season—March to September, or later in the Deep South—enormous congresses assemble in ponds or temporary pools, where they advertise their presence with their trademark nasal call and engage in a good deal of elbowing and pushing during aquatic courtship. When a male "achieves the favored position," Smithsonian curator Doris Cochran once observed, he clasps his forearms around the female's body and presses his chin "closely against her back." Yet even as the eggs are being fertilized and released, "the intimacy of the moment [is] not respected, for other frogs now clamor all about, and this pair [is] thumped and bumped in no gentle fashion." The entire riverbank "seethes with creative furor," she adds, in "mindless obedience to an instinct that insured the continuance of the race."

Green Tree Frog
Hyla cinerea

Green tree frogs are only about 1.25–2.50 inches (31–62 mm) long, but the span of their jump has been measured at an astonishing 8–10 feet (2.40–3 meters).

Gray Tree Frog
Hyla versicolor, Hyla chrysoscelis

For years, two lookalike species of gray tree frog (a.k.a. the Northern tree toad, common tree toad, changeable tree toad, and chameleon hyla) have "masqueraded" as one. Only by studying their voices and chromosomes, Roger Conant and Joseph Collins explain, can *Hyla versicolor* (the common gray tree frog) and *Hyla chrysoscelis* (Cope's tree frog) be distinguished. "For practical purposes," they conclude, "it is sufficient to identify either species as a gray tree frog."

Widespread use of the common name "tree *toad*" points to something peculiar about these rather plump-looking tree frogs: Their skin has a rough, granular, even warty appearance (helping to dispel the myth "that all frogs are smooth and all toads are warty," Thomas Tyning asserts). The skin color varies considerably from brown to greenish gray, with bright orange on the undersurfaces of the hind legs and darker starlike markings or blotches—"shaped like a Rorshach inkblot design," Porter suggests—on the frog's back. The overall effect is a masterful disguise that harmonizes perfectly with lichen and with the rough bark of gray birch and other trees. The frog's shining black horizontal pupils are set against a grayish green, chocolate, or flame-colored iris reticulated with a rich networking of black lines.

The gray tree frog's extremes in color change—and the speed with which it can transform itself—have long fascinated observers and given rise to some of the common names noted above. These color changes, light or dark, "are caused by the change in the shape of the pigment cells," Porter explains. "Such changes may be brought on by various stimuli to the tree frog, both external and internal. Low tem-peratures cause its pigment to expand and its skin to assume a dark color, but high temperatures produce the opposite effect. Bright light will cause the skin to turn pale, while subdued light or darkness causes the color to darken."

Curiously, when gray tree frog tadpoles emerge from the water as froglets, they are a bright shade of emerald-green. "Evidently," Smyth says, "it is to the froglet's advantage to be green as it journeys from the pond through green grass to the tree."

Gray tree frogs are common east of the Great Plains, from Maine to northern Florida, but are seldom seen except during the breeding season—preferring to remain out of sight in woodland trees or shrubs, sleeping by day and catching insects by night. When glimpsed near suburban or rural homes, perched in tree cavities, hollow stumps, or along stone walls, wooden fences, and decks, these frogs are often found in the same location day after day, sometimes for weeks at a time.

When the mating season approaches, generally April to August, the males seek out shallow ponds or creeks and begin to sing. Their advertisement call is a short, resonant trill, lower pitched and of shorter duration than that of the American toad. At dusk or during a rain storm, Dickerson writes, "the sound has the charm of contentment in it; in fact, it is much like the purring of a cat only louder. At a distance, it sounds something like the bleating of a lamb." The frog first inflates its single vocal sac and then issues an explosive series of trills, vibrating its entire body "like a riveter," observes Porter.

Males stake out territories of about 30 inches (750 mm) or more from one another and engage in brief wrestling bouts if necessary to drive off male trespassers. Sometimes a "satellite male" will position

Gray tree frog
Observers note that gray tree frogs frequently return day after day to the same resting place, favoring hollow stumps and tree cavities.

himself a foot or two from a singing male, hoping to intercept a female or lay claim to the spot when the vocalist leaves with a mate. Tyning reports that a female will walk, rather than hop, to a calling male, then touch him with her nose "or actually leap upon him." During amplexus, the female lays up to two thousand eggs, attached singly or in small groups to vegetation at the surface of or beneath the water. The tadpoles, which produce a toxic secretion, are easily recognized by their bright orange or scarlet tails, presumably a warning signal to predators.

Gray tree frogs usually hibernate on the ground beneath fallen leaves or in crevices and are sometimes encountered by late-season gardeners planting bulbs or shrubs. Like wood frogs, spring peepers, and striped chorus frogs, they have an amazing capacity to withstand subfreezing temperatures—to as low as -20 degrees F (-28.9 degrees C), according to Kenneth and Janet Storey—by manufacturing glycerol in their blood.

Juvenile and adult gray tree frogs are popular subjects for observation (when they're not sleeping) for their enthusiastic displays of acrobatics. Unlike many other frogs, they are not particularly nervous around humans, and their large toe discs offer a showman's ability to adhere to tree limbs or glass when in pursuit of a meal. Unfortunately, their aim is not always true, although, as Smyth observes, this lends them a personality ("confiding and clumsy") even if they miss their target.

Gray Tree Frog
Hyla versicolor, Hyla chrysoscelis

Gray tree frog
The skin of a gray tree frog is much rougher than that of other tree frogs, which explains why this species is often called a "tree toad."

Gray tree frogs have an amazing capacity to withstand subfreezing temperatures—to as low as -20 degrees F (-28.9 degrees C)—by manufacturing glycerol in their blood.

Barking Tree Frog
Hyla gratiosa

North America's largest native tree frog acquired its name as a result of its raucous and explosive call—a harsh *arrk-arrk-arrk-arrk* advertisement call that can sound like a pack of hounds.

The male barking tree frog (*Hyla gratiosa*) varies his call depending on whether he is calling from water ("a hollow, resonant *ooonk-ooonk-ooonk*," according to Lang Elliott) or barking from shrubs or treetops. Ranging from Virginia to Florida and Louisiana, with some isolated colonies in Delaware, Maryland, Kentucky, Tennessee and perhaps New Jersey, this plump tree frog has a skin texture unlike that of any other American species. Neither smoothly textured nor rough and warty, this frog has a thick, leathery skin with fine granulation over the upper parts, giving it what Dickerson calls "a curiously artificial look." The skin color is usually leaf-green, brown, or gray, with small, dark blotches or lemon-yellow spots. Changes in color can be quite rapid, and the spots, too, seem to disappear and reappear over time. The frog's eyes are reddish bronze or gold with black, and the throat is bright green or yellow (in the male) or purplish brown (in the female).

The barking tree frog ranges in size from about 2–2.75 inches (50–69 mm); its head is fairly broad and pug-like, and the disks on its fingers and toes are quite large. In fact, these frogs are the "clowns of the amphibian world," Cochran says, and can be trained to swing on toy trapezes in captivity like miniature acrobats.

Barking tree frogs spend the warm summer months in the upper branches of pine barrens, hammocks, and stands of live oak. In the winter, or during dry periods, they burrow into the soil around tree roots or vegetation in search of moisture. During the breeding season, they gather in cypress swamps or by ponds to lay their eggs at the bottom of pools of water. In Gainesville, Florida, the first choruses of barking tree frogs would traditionally assemble in the water aerator of the city's power plant, according to Carr, where the water was "abnormally warm" and where insects were attracted to the electric lights.

Barking tree frog
This frog is readily identified by the dark rounded spots on its back. In Gainesville, Florida, the first choruses of these raucous tree frogs traditionally assemble in the power plant's water aerator, where temperatures are warmer and electric lights attract insects.

Barking Tree Frog
Hyla gratiosa

Squirrel Tree Frog
Hyla squirella

Squirrel Tree Frog
Hyla squirella

The squirrel tree frog of the southeastern United States could have been named for its remarkable treetop acrobatics, or for its propensity for scrambling across rooftops—but it wasn't. Instead, *Hyla squirella* was named for its rain call, which sounds curiously like the scolding or chattering of a squirrel.

The raspy rain call isn't this frog's only unusual vocalization; its breeding call is distinctive, too—characterized by Conant and Collins as "Morse code done with a snore—no messages, but with the abandon of an amateur playing with a telegraph key." When squirrel tree frogs call in large choruses, the authors add, they sound like "a series of riveting machines all operating at once."

Squirrel tree frogs are small (roughly 0.875–1.75 inches, or 22–44 mm, long) and smooth-skinned, and their rapid color changes never cease to amaze observers. Dickerson concluded that light, moisture, and temperature all were factors affecting the tree frog's color, but she also discovered that changes in skin color continued in the field even when conditions did not change. Usually green or brown, often with small yellow or white spots and a light stripe over the jaw and along the side, this frog is hard to see in the wild and even more difficult to catch. Collectors characterize it as an energetic jumper, and, after opening a box of squirrel tree frogs on a collecting expedition, "we lose most of them the moment they are uncovered," Dickerson reports. "They do not wait to be lifted out. . . . They jump simultaneously . . . all in different directions."

Squirrel tree frogs are nocturnal, sleeping by day in pine flatwoods, oak trees, or palmettos near cypress swamps, wells, fields, or gardens, and hunting insects by night. When studying the amphibians in her Florida yard, Olive Goin noticed that squirrel tree frogs would habitually return day after day to the underside of the same leaf to sleep, carefully tucking their front feet under their chins. In fact, Goin found these tree frogs (which she called "rain frogs," one of their several southern nicknames) in more than just her trees and shrubs—she also repeatedly found them inside her house.

"They get on the roof and fall down the chimney," Goin explained, "and many a time, after hearing a soft thump in the fireplace, I have picked up a dusty, sooty little rain frog, washed it off, and put it back outdoors."

Ranging from the coastal plains of Virginia south to Florida and west to central Texas, squirrel tree frogs breed from April to August in northern areas and March to October farther south. The advertisement call of the male is characterized by Lang Elliott as a "nasal, buzzing *rrrraak-rrrraak-rrrraak*"; Archie Carr calls it "rather ventriloquistic; flat; short to Italian *a*; *aaaa* or *waaaaak*." Performed from the shallow waters of ponds or rain-filled ditches, this vocalization has less staying power than the songs of other species, but the scolding, chattering quack of the rain call is far more widely recognized throughout the South—the choral trademark performed just before a summer shower.

*T*he scolding, chattering quack of the squirrel tree frog's rain call is recognized throughout the American South as its choral trademark, performed just before a summer shower.

Squirrel tree frog
Easily mistaken for a green tree frog, the squirrel tree frog, or "rain frog," is a quick-change artist, capable of transforming its skin color from green to brown or back in a flash. Squirrel tree frogs sometimes tumble down chimneys and fall out of trees while chasing insects.

In the American North, the spring peeper is a true harbinger of spring, waking as early as February and singing in choruses from March to May or June as the first warm rains fall.

Spring peeper

When a male spring peeper inflates his transparent throat and sings, his sharp, high-pitched pe-ep, pe-ep *sounds like a bird, a whistle, or sleigh bells. In large choruses, the ear-splitting jangle of these frogs can be deafening.*

Spring Peeper
Pseudacris crucifer

To residents of the Deep South, there is something downright odd about applying the name "spring peeper" to *Pseudacris* (formerly *Hyla*) *crucifer*, since this frog begins singing as early as November, and, as Olive Goin points out, "they are always sounding forth in full chorus by Christmas time." (In Florida, she insists, they should be called "winter peepers.")

To Northerners, however, this frog is one of the true harbingers of spring, waking as early as February and singing in choruses from March to May or June as the first warm rains begin to fall. If the species' common name seems inappropriate to some, at least the scientific name is apt: *crucifer* is the Latin word for "cross-bearing"—a reference to the large mark resembling an "X" or cross on the peeper's back. (To a filmgoer, this "X" also pro-

vides a convenient reminder of the frog's name, since "peepers" have an affinity for X-rated movies.)

Whatever its label, this little tree frog clearly merits the latter half of its name, for it sings its heart out with a sharp, high-pitched, birdlike *pe-ep, pe-ep, pe-ep*, which sounds like the jingle of sleigh bells when heard from a distance. In choruses, the effect of so many voices singing together can be "almost ear-splitting," Dickerson remarks, audible up to a mile away.

Goin's meticulous journal observations of the reptiles and amphibians around her Gainesville home produced one particularly remarkable revelation: A chorus of spring peepers "is not a lot of frogs all sounding forth at the same time"; rather, it is a number of trios, each singing in a particular musical sequence.

"One frog starts things off by sounding the note of A a number of times," Goin writes. "If he is not answered, he pauses and gives a little trill. Usually this stimulates another frog to respond with a G#, and the two call back and forth. . . . Now the last member of the trio chimes in with a B, and so they continue: A, G#, B; A, G#, B; A, G#, B. A full chorus is made up of many of these tiny independent trios, each frog apparently ignoring all others save the two with which it is singing."

In the North, these tiny peepers (0.75–1.50 inches or 19–38 mm) emerge from their woodland hibernation sites under the soil or beneath logs, leaves, and bark and migrate to ponds and flooded meadows to begin their singing. According to Kenneth and Janet Storey, these frogs survive the icy cold by manufacturing glucose, which limits dehydration and prevents cell damage. Since they emerge so early, spring peepers may find little to eat, so they must rely on stored reserves of fat. As the days begin to warm, however, an array of insect prey—gnats, flies, ants, mosquitoes—provides a source of food for the hungry frogs.

Male callers far outnumber female frogs at the spawning sites, sometimes by a ratio of 9:1. (By fall, however, that ratio will be closer to 1:1, according to H.R. Heusser, after automobiles and normal predation have taken their toll.) The fawn-colored, tan, reddish brown, or olive-gray males, like most other frogs of their sex, are characteristically smaller than their female counterparts; what helps the females to distinguish the more "fit" and reproductively superior prospective mates, current research suggests, may be the speed of their calls—since males that are larger and older "tend to call at a much faster rate than smaller (and younger) males," Tyning says.

The male inflates his vocal sac to "enormous proportions," observes Cochran, "so that it projects far in front of his chest like a balloon." As air is inhaled, crossing the vocal cords, it produces the call, which is amplified in the peeper's round, flesh-colored vocal sac. The callers themselves are nearly impossible to spot, since "all voices suddenly cease at your footsteps," Cochran says. However, if you stand "perfectly still for a few minutes, the very short memories of the frogs lose the image of you as a moving creature and they consider you no more than a tree stump or other fixed object." Should they wish to escape, or merely catch a meal, peepers can jump remarkable lengths, reportedly seventeen times their own body length—the equivalent of a human jumping more than 100 feet (30 meters).

After a female is enticed to a pond or pool of standing water by the males' choral concerts, she will swim toward a prospective mate and touch him. The male then hops on her back and clasps her in the amplexus position, leaving the swimming to her. The female lays up to one thousand eggs, attached individually or in small clusters to the stems of plants, before exiting the water and returning to the woods.

After the tadpoles hatch and transform into froglets, the little peepers may exhibit signs of gregariousness, forming groups and traveling about in successive waves of emergence, their main interest in life hunting for food.

Sometimes smaller "satellite males" take up positions in the vicinity of calling males, maintaining a "low posture, holding their heads down close to their feet," Tyning reports. But interception of females apparently is not their primary objective; instead, they wait for the resident male to leave his territory to engage in copulation, then lay claim to his turf and begin their own calling.

Spring Peeper
Pseudacris crucifer

Cuban Tree Frog
Osteopilus septentrionalis

Several decades ago, while a generation of jittery Americans was nervously anticipating an "invasion" of the United States by forces from Fidel Castro's Cuba, native Floridians were already experiencing the real thing—from Cuban tree frogs.

The Cuban, or giant, tree frog (*Osteopilus septentrionalis*) began arriving in Key West sometime early in the century in shipments of vegetables and fruit from Cuba. A native of the West Indies, this hitchhiker remained limited to the Florida Keys and Dade County until the late 1960s, when it spread northward into central Florida by hiding in produce crates and on nursery stock.

These transplanted frogs, variably colored olive-brown, bronze, or gray, were relative giants compared to native American tree frogs, sometimes growing to a record 5.50 inches (138 mm). They not only demonstrated an insatiable appetite for cockroaches, crickets, and other insects, they also began preying on local populations of green and squirrel tree frogs. In fact, a Cuban tree frog will eat just about anything it can catch; in captivity, it readily devours its fellow frogs and may turn cannibalistic.

As North America's largest tree frog, this amphibian is easily identified by its enormous size, large toepads, rough, warty skin, glowing orange-tinted eyes, and its irascibility when handled. Photographer John Netherton recalls he had to "wrestle" with a pair of Cuban tree frogs when attempting to remove them from a shipping box—and the ghastly stench that emanated from their jar at feeding time was surely one of the most vile we ever smelled. Newly captured specimens exude copious quantities of a secretion that can be quite irritating to humans.

In southern Florida, Cuban tree frogs are regular visitors to suburban homes, frequenting patios and porches where container plants are watered regularly and clinging to screen windows and sliding glass doors. At night, they sometimes gather around streetlights in search of insects, and they find billboards especially attractive sites for catching bugs drawn to the bright lights.

After frog enthusiast George Porter began hearing rumors in the 1960s that Cuban tree frogs were causing power failures in Florida, he checked with Florida Power and Light and came across this item in the firm's newsletter:

"Tree frogs have added to FPL maintenance problems. . . . Croakers hop up poles, straddle two wires on small transformers and cause them to short out. . . . The frogs only climb when temperatures range between 55 and 75 degrees F [12.8 and 23.9 degrees C]. And these climbers are usually the spouseless frogs. 'Squirrel guards' on the poles have proven to be an effective deterrent."

From May to October, "spouseless" males advertise their presence with a call described as a rasping snarl. (Albert and Anna Wright compare it to the sound of a rope being pulled through an unoiled pulley.) Females lay their eggs in ponds, lakes, swimming pools, and the flooded basements of abandoned buildings. Cisterns, which abounded in the Florida Keys before Franklin Roosevelt's New Deal but are now ramshackle and neglected, are especially popular as breeding sites.

Cuban tree frog, right, and green tree frog
The Cuban tree frog, accidentally introduced to Key West and Florida in shipments of produce from Cuba, is America's largest tree frog. This Cuban tree frog hungrily eyes a smaller green tree frog, one of several native species whose populations in the Everglades and elsewhere have been ravaged by the larger, more aggressive Cuban immigrants.

Cuban Tree Frog
Osteopilus septentrionalis

*C*uban tree frogs have an insatiable appetite for cockroaches, crickets, and other insects—and can become cannibals in captivity, preying on fellow tree frogs.

White's tree frog
The bluish green skin of the White's tree frog of Australia has a distinctly waxy appearance, and rolling folds of skin are usually visible above the tympanum. This species is remarkably tame; its tendency to grow plump in captivity has earned it the nickname "dumpy tree frog."

*I*n 1992, chemists and zoologists reported that the White's tree frog exudes a compound that destroys a staph bacterium responsible for abscesses and that is active against the cold-sore virus *Herpes simplex*; a peptide called caerulein from the frog's skin secretions lowers human blood pressure.

White's Tree Frog
Litoria caerulea

Of the more than 150 species of tree frogs currently identified in Australia and New Guinea, White's tree frog—first described in 1790 in J. White's *Journal of a Voyage to New South Wales*—is probably the most famous and popular. It is widely celebrated for its waxy green-blue appearance and rolling folds of skin, which look like slabs of fat and have earned the frog the ungallant nickname "dumpy frog." Its popularity is due mainly to a trusting and tranquil disposition in captivity.

White's tree frog (*Litoria caerulea*) is found throughout southern New Guinea and northern and eastern Australia, where it has not been affected as adversely by the predatory cane toad as have so many other species of frogs, says Australian herpetologist Raymond Hoser.

Seldom shy around humans, White's tree frog is commonplace around human habitation, especially lavatories, water tanks, garden ponds, and city water reservoirs. During the summer months, these mainly (but not exclusively) nocturnal creatures show up on verandas and brazenly enter homes in search of moisture and food. (The tamer visitors have even been known to accept food from a person's fingers.) White's tree frogs average 2–4 inches (50–100 mm) in length, though larger specimens, upwards of 6 inches (150 mm), can be found in Queensland. Its broad toepads are large and sticky, capable of supporting the rotund frog as it searches for moths, locusts, roaches, and other insects.

The deep, throaty call of this tree frog is a distinctive *wark-wark-wark*. Breeding takes place during the summer and wet season in drainage systems, water tanks, or semi-permanent swamps; females deposit clutches of two hundred to three hundred eggs that promptly hatch within twenty-four hours.

While most observers regard the White's tree frog as simply an interesting or eccentric variety of herpetofauna, its possible contributions to science may one day prove considerable. In 1992, chemists and zoologists at the University of Adelaide studying skin secretions from this tree frog and two other species reported that the frogs exude a compound that can destroy a staph bacterium responsible for abscesses and that is active against the cold-sore virus *Herpes simplex*. The scientists also discovered that a peptide called caerulein, isolated from the skin secretions and identified in previous research, can lower human blood pressure.

"As the list of possible pharmaceutical products extracted from amphibians grows," Bradley Smith concluded in his review of the Australian findings, "it seems that amphibians are carrying a potential medicine chest on their backs."

Bullfrog
Rana catesbeiana

There's a scene in the 1972 film *Frogs* in which a wave of mutant frogs and toads (whose genes have gone berserk, thanks to pollutants dumped into the water by Southern tycoon Ray Milland) emerge from the toxic swampwaters and begin to storm the family plantation.

Which species of frog did Hollywood cast as the most menacing marauder? The bullfrog, of course—North America's largest native species of frog (or so the characters in the movie claim; in reality, the filmmakers rely primarily on cane toads).

Bullfrogs were a logical choice: They range from about 3.50–6 inches (88–150 mm) in length; the record is 8 inches (250 mm). And they weigh up to a record 1 pound, 4 ounces (0.560 kg); the *Guinness Book of Animal Facts and Feats* cites an "outsized freak" caught in Washington state in 1949 that allegedly weighed 7 pounds, 4 ounces (3.25 kg). Florida's cane toads grow larger than bullfrogs, but they are an introduced species and not native to the United States.

Bullfrogs are big frogs, all right, yet their name comes not from their beefy bulk but, rather, from their extraordinary voice. The vibrant bass notes of a bullfrog remind listeners of the bellowing of a bull—a foghornlike reverberation audible up to half a mile away. Many people claim to hear the words *jug-o'-rum, jug-o'-rum, jug-o'-rum* in the bullfrog's deep-pitched call, or sometimes *more rum*, or *be drowned*, or *better go round*.

The frog's musical prowess, Dickerson recalls, was once demonstrated during a rehearsal of a women's chorus: A large bullfrog in an adjoining room "began vigorously ejaculating, 'Jug o' rum, jug o' rum, jug o' rum,' . . . [and] the first few notes of the frog were in time and harmony with the chords of the selection."

However characterized, the call of the male bullfrog does more than just signal sex and species or advertise territory and readiness to mate—it also attracts humans in search of a gourmet delight. Over the course of many centuries, frogs' legs have earned a reputation for their delicate flavor, and bullfrog legs in particular have achieved gastronomic popularity due to their size. As a consequence, the bullfrog's fleshy bulk and bistro value have inspired both widespread "frogging" (catching frogs by night, armed with a flashlight and gig or spear) and bullfrog "farming."

"There is a market right in your vicinity for all the frogs you raise," Florida agriculture officials pronounced in the '50s. "Hotels and restaurants pay good prices . . . if you just advertise and educate the people to the food value and good taste of the giant bullfrog."

*B*ullfrogs weigh up to a record 1 pound, 4 ounces (0.560 kg); the *Guinness Book of Animal Facts and Feats* cites an "outsized freak" caught in Washington state in 1949 that weighed 7 pounds, 4 ounces (3.25 kg).

Bullfrog
A bullfrog will remain motionless for hours at a time in duckweed or other water plants, poised to snatch at any insects, snakes, small birds, or other frogs that stray in its direction.

Bullfrog
Rana Catesbeiana

Bullfrog tadpole
A bullfrog tadpole will sprout all four legs before the process of absorbing its tail is complete. Sometimes one of these tadpoles will venture out of water, looking like a strange cross between a frog and a salamander.

Good taste aside, the bullfrog ranks high in popularity for other reasons as well. For one thing, it is often a star performer at frog-jumping contests, even though the green frog and tiny cricket frog can actually jump farther. Then, too, a bullfrog can live to a remarkably ripe old age (twenty-five to thirty years); its physical characteristics and habits are beguiling; and its appetite can assume Falstaffian proportions.

In the wild, bullfrogs are loners. They take up residence in lakes and ponds, where they expose their broad head, goggle eyes, and snout just above the surface of the water and wait for their next meal to happen along. Larger, older males will stake out territories from 6–20 feet (1.80–6 meters) in diameter and challenge or attack other males that intrude; smaller "satellite males" may move in near a singing male in hopes of intercepting females attracted by the dominant male's lusty calls.

Bullfrogs are usually drab green, olive, or brownish black, with random mottling of dark spots and barred legs; occasionally, individuals will sport yellow, albino, or even blue skin coloration. The undersides are light (though usually mottled), and males have yellow throats and prominent eardrums that are larger than their eyes.

Equipped with powerful hind legs, these frogs are good leapers and divers and are especially fine swimmers. The frog's nostrils are closed underwater, and its eyes are shut and lowered into the sockets when swimming. "This takes the eyes out of danger," Dickerson notes, but it may also inhibit the distance the frog will swim.

At breeding time, males may resort to butting, wrestling, or shouldering one another and splashing around a good deal when engaged in territorial combat. If seized by a large predator, a bullfrog may go limp and "play possum," Stebbins says, then spring to life after the attacker is lulled into complacency.

Breeding takes place February through July, and eggs are laid in huge floating masses of more than twenty thousand eggs. Curiously, in the North, bullfrog tadpoles take considerably longer to metamorphose than those of most other species, overwintering for up to two years before emerging as a frog.

The eating habits of bullfrogs are legendary. Relying on its quick tongue and awesomely large mouth, the bullfrog will snatch up insects, fish, crayfish, turtles, frogs (even of the same species), birds, and even small ducks. In fact, Dickerson says, a bullfrog will eat "any moving object that he can swallow or partially swallow." Sometimes a bullfrog is both predator and prey: A large bullfrog, for example, "will eat a small water snake," Porter explains, while "a large water snake will eat a small bullfrog." In addition to snakes and man, other threats to this frog include hungry alligators, snapping turtles, raccoons, otters, and herons.

The introduction of bullfrogs to regions where they are not indigenous has had a devastating impact on local amphibians, reptiles, and other animals. Although bullfrogs were once common only in the East, South, and Central United States, they are now found west of the Rockies, as well as in Hawaii, Mexico, Jamaica, Italy, and Japan. The Japanese frogs trace their ancestry back to a shipment of five thousand American bullfrogs that escaped from breeding pens sometime in the late 1930s. The copulatory zeal of these American imports helped the bullfrog to become "a national dish" in the Land of Flowers.

Northern and Southern Leopard Frog

Rana pipiens, Rana utricularia

Leopard frogs—long-legged jumpers of the meadows identified by the rounded spots on their backs—have been called the most beautiful of North American common frogs, though some confusion still exists regarding their classification into species and subspecies. Best known are the Northern leopard frog (*Rana pipiens*) and Southern leopard frog (*Rana utricularia*), both of which are routinely confused with their cousin the pickerel frog, whose spots are more square-shaped and arranged in parallel rows down the back.

Due to its widespread range, the Northern leopard frog has acquired a variety of regional nicknames over the years, including meadow frog, grass frog, peeping frog, shad frog, and herring hopper. Common across North America from Canada south to Kentucky and west to the Pacific and Southwest states, the Northern leopard grows roughly 2–4.375 inches (50–109 mm) in length (not including the legs) and sports a metallic green or brown livery adorned with two or three rows of round or oval spots randomly situated between a pair of ridges. These "leopard-like" spots, appearing on the back and also on the sides, are usually dark with light borders and occasionally run together. The frog's striking eyes are orange-gold with black horizontal pupils.

According to Dickerson, leopard frogs of the eastern United States are smoother and more slender, while their southern and western counterparts are rougher-skinned and much more "robust" in build. Leopard frogs are "very handsome and alert-looking," she insists, and their young are "aristocratic" in appearance. (Their pickled brethren are widely used in biology classrooms across

the nation to introduce young scholars to the art of dissection. Sometimes, as in Steven Spielberg's film *E.T.,* the luckier ones escape.)

Though primarily nocturnal, the Northern leopard frog is frequently encountered by day during the summer months in grasslands and hay fields, and it is found in the woodlands and higher mountain forests of the West. Stebbins says this frog forages far from water in damper meadowlands, and, "when frightened on land, it often seeks water in a series of zigzag jumps." A good jumper can leap as far as 6 feet (1.80 meters), according to Halliday and Adler, "which is 15 times their body length." Besides being difficult to catch, leopard frogs also squirt a disagreeable-smelling liquid into the face of would-be captors or predators before executing a quick retreat.

The voice of the Northern leopard frog is characterized by a throaty, low-pitched snoring sound (sometimes likened to the noise of a motorboat engine

Southern leopard frog
The leopard frog has an alert expression and prominent leopard-like spots on its body and legs. Unlike most other species, female leopard frogs are able to sing, though not as loudly as their male counterparts.

Northern Leopard Frog
Rana pipiens

Southern leopard frog

The Southern leopard frog has many enemies, including herons, raccoons, turtles, and alligators. On land, a cornered leopard frog often squirts a disagreeable-smelling liquid into a predator's face before leaping to safety.

Southern Leopard Frog
Rana utricularia

or a woodpecker tapping on a dead tree), interspersed with clucking or grunts. Choruses can produce "a medley of moaning, grunting, and chuckling," Stebbins notes, suggestive of "the sounds made by rubbing a well-inflated rubber balloon." In early spring, American swamps come alive with the music of these frogs, the invisible callers sometimes singing beneath the surface of the water. If disturbed at the edge of their breeding pond, these frogs often squawk as they leap toward the water; if caught, they may even scream. Dickerson, however, once kept a tame leopard frog that would sing "in low purring tones" when she poured water on his back.

Researchers report that a female leopard frog often approaches a male and touches him to initiate amplexus. On the other hand, a male leopard frog will in-

discriminately grasp another frog, according to Halliday and Adler, before identifying the gender of his partner by touch (females will be swollen with eggs) or by voice. If the male happens to clasp another male, the object of his passion will express his displeasure by uttering a warning call.

Females deposit as many as five thousand to six thousand tiny eggs in elongated masses (reaching up to 6 feet, or 1.80 meters, in length), attaching them to small sticks, cattails, or submerged vegetation in communal breeding sites. Tadpoles hatch nine to ten days later and begin nibbling on weeds, green pond slime, and other detritus. The diet of juvenile and adult leopard frogs consists chiefly of crickets, grasshoppers, spiders, and worms. Although it is the flying or crawling movements of bugs that attract the frog's attention, recent studies suggest that leopard frogs can also locate prey by using their sense of smell.

Like its northern brother, the Southern leopard frog is a slender, medium-sized frog (2–5 inches or 50–125 mm) with rounded or oval spots randomly distributed on its back and sides. Although this frog is generally green or brown (or some combination of the two), its spots lack the surrounding light rings that appear on the northern variety. Conant and Collins say the southern species has a longer, more pointed head, fewer dark spots on its sides, and often a distinct white or yellow spot in the middle of the tympanum. In the Florida Keys, it has a bronze-colored throat and mottled undersides.

The Southern leopard frog, which ranges from southern New York to the Florida Keys and west through Texas to Oklahoma and Kansas, frequents shallow freshwater habitats but tolerates brackish marshlands along the coasts. During the summer it can be found wandering afield, where it may be called the "grass frog" because of frequent appearances in grassy and weedy areas.

In his book about the Everglades, Archie Carr says this frog "is a superior animal, alert, sharp-faced, great at hurdling across broken country." Its unusually long hind legs are a great asset for escaping predators such as herons and raccoons, and when it dives into the water, it often makes sharp turns before surfacing. The call of the Southern leopard frog has been described as a series of chuckles or throaty croaks or even like a hand scratching a tightly blown balloon.

Pickerel Frog
Rana palustris

Widely regarded as the "twin brother" of the leopard frog, the North American pickerel frog (*Rana palustris*) has confused many an amateur naturalist attempting to identify it, since both species sport prominent spots on their backs. The difference between the two may be subtle, but it's a reliable indicator in the field: The leopard frog's spots are round (or oval), while the pickerel frog's are rectangular or square-shaped.

The pickerel frog is prized by fishermen as a freshwater bait, which apparently accounts for its name (large pickerel and walleyed pike will feed on this species). In addition, both the frog and pike can be found in the vicinity of pickerelweed, a blue-flowering aquatic plant that grows in shallow water.

The pickerel frog, common along the Atlantic seaboard and in the upper Midwest, ranges from Canada southward to the Carolinas and westward to Minnesota and Texas. In the North, it is found in the cool, clear waters of spring lakes, running streams, and sphagnum bogs; in the South, it frequents the waters of swamps and coastal plains. Although pickerel frogs are more likely to remain close to water than leopard frogs, they too are often glimpsed in meadows, fields, and rocky ravines in search of insects or en route to water to escape enemies or lay eggs. Explorers even encounter pickerel frogs at the entrances to caves.

Herpetologists who collect pickerel frogs warn of their toxic skin-gland secretions, which make the species unappetizing to most predators—and an agent of death to other frogs housed in the same collecting jar. Hungry garter snakes and water snakes will refuse to eat a pickerel frog (which secretes an irritating fluid in the snake's mouth); bullfrogs, on the other hand, apparently regard pickerel frogs as just another meal and eat them without apparent distress. Izaak Walton claimed in *The Compleat Angler* that pike

*T*he pickerel frog is prized by fishermen as freshwater bait for pickerel and walleyed pike, which is believed to account for the frog's name.

Pickerel frog
Because the pickerel frog has large dark spots on its back, it is often mistaken for a leopard frog. The pickerel frog's spots are squarish, however, rather than round and are arranged in parallel rows down the frog's back.

83

Pickerel Frog
Rana palustris

Pickerel frog
Pickerel frogs spend most of their lives out of water, venturing into meadows and fields in search of food. These frogs are avoided by most snakes and mammals because of their unpleasant-tasting glandular secretions.

eat a venomous frog only after killing it and washing it thoroughly by tumbling the frog up and down in the water.

The advertisement call of the male pickerel frog is a harsh snore or rolling croak, sometimes emanating from underwater. Dickerson says the call resembles the sound "produced in tearing resisting cloth of some sort"; the pitch, she adds, is always low—ranging "from G to A below Middle C."

Females lay their eggs in shallow water from March to May and sometimes enlist their consorts to kick other males away. Irregular masses of two thousand to three thousand brownish eggs are attached to stems of aquatic plants or submerged twigs. After metamorphosis, young pickerel frogs exhibit bright coats that often eclipse the livery of their typically greenish brown or tan parents. (No

other frog presents a coat "of so brilliant a metallic lustre [of] shining gold and bronze," Dickerson insists.) The rectangular spots, which lack the light-colored rims found on leopard frogs, appear in parallel rows down the back, and distinctive flashes of orange or yellow can be seen on the undersides of the hind legs. Adult frogs are smooth-skinned, average about 2–3 inches (50–75 mm) in length, and feed chiefly on flies, caterpillars, butterflies, beetles, and other insects.

Wood Frog
Rana sylvatica

To a native of the Midwest, the wood frog (*Rana sylvatica*) is the region's most handsome frog. What distinguishes this fine fellow from his Ranid relatives is the color of his skin—a rich reddish brown, garnished with a dark-brown mask (other

Midwestern "true frogs" are generally green or spotted). What also makes this frog unique is its unusually early spring breeding season, its preference for woodland habitats, and its peculiar *cack-a-hack* advertisement call.

Curiously, the wood frog's trademark brown hue varies widely; adult frogs range from "sunset pink," tan, and fawn-color to olive, chocolate-brown, and black. The dark, raccoonlike "robber's mask" extends behind the tympanum, dark blotches sometimes appear on the glistening white or cream-colored chest, and crossbars are often visible on the legs.

"The wood frog is beautiful at all times," Dickerson declares. "It has a high-bred and a delicate air"; its eyes are "very prominent and possess an alert but gentle expression"; and "its appearance and ways are always in harmony with the subdued light." In fact, the wood frog's varying shades of brown, its mask, and barred legs blend in exceptionally well with leaf litter on the forest floor, and the frog can change its shade from light to dark (or vice versa) in just fifteen minutes.

Wood frogs dwell chiefly in mixed woodlands and shady forests, except when venturing to and from ponds or standing pools in the early spring to breed; in the colder regions, they are sometimes found in open grassy areas. The wood frog is distributed widely throughout the northeast and Great Lakes states, ranging west to Arkansas and Missouri (with isolated colonies in northern Colorado and the Big Horn Mountains of Wyoming) and as far south as northern Georgia and central Alabama. But it is the species' astonishing northern range—throughout Labrador to Alaska's Brooks Mountains in the Arctic Circle— that gives this frog claim to the title of this continent's northernmost species.

Since life on the tundra creates serious survival problems for a cold-blooded animal, the wood frog has had to adapt. Its solution is to manufacture "antifreeze" compounds in its body—i.e., massive quantities of glucose—to fight off the freezing cold during hibernation. Biochemists Kenneth and Janet Storey report that ice on the wood frog's skin triggers "a hormonal or nervous response that instantly activates glycogen breakdown in the liver, flooding glucose into the blood." While most amphibians seek (warmer) hibernation sites at the bottom of ponds or deep under the earth, wood frogs can survive the effects of sub-zero temperatures beneath logs, rocks, or leaf litter with up to 65 percent of their body water frozen to ice.

It should come as no surprise, then, that the wood frog emerges first from

*T*he wood frog manufactures "antifreeze" compounds in its body in the form of glucose to fight off the freezing cold during hibernation on the tundra.

Wood frog
The wood frog is a handsomely colored woodland species, generally brown or gray, with a pointed snout and dark mask over its eyes and cheeks. Wood frogs are usually the first to emerge from hibernation, sometimes as early as February, laying their eggs in masses that can survive freezing in ponds and temporary pools.

Wood Frog
Rana sylvatica

hibernation—sometimes as early as February, when temperatures hover around freezing—to begin its trek to nearby ponds or ditches of standing water in search of a mate. Henry David Thoreau characterized the call of the wood frog as *"Wurrk wurrk wurr r k wurk"*; frog-call expert Lang Elliott describes the repetitive ducklike quacking as a series of harsh *cack-a-hack-a-hack* or *r-r-racket* notes. Male wood frogs call while floating in or swimming under the water; when a female enters the water, her swimming movements attract the attention of excited males. Sex recognition is achieved by "trial embrace," Smyth explains: "All nearby moving objects are seized," and "those which croak or whose bodies are not of sufficient girth are released immediately."

Albert Wright recalls crawling on his belly to the edge of a pond in Ithaca, New York, in 1908 to observe several hundred male wood frogs croaking lustily. "It resembled a small toad concourse," he re-

members, with considerable "scrabbling and zeal of mating. When I arose, the frogs all disappeared simultaneously."

Female wood frogs lay their eggs in masses of one thousand to three thousand, sometimes attached to sticks or reeds in shallow water. In the days that follow, the jelly-encased masses turn green, due to the presence of microscopic algae that feed on carbon dioxide generated by the tiny tadpoles. The greenish olive or black hatchlings first feed on the masses of jelly, then later may nibble on other tadpoles' tails. Toxins in the skin develop early, Tyning says, making the tadpoles distasteful to many aquatic predators.

After adults leave the breeding ponds to return to their woodland habitats, their "postnuptial" dark copper-brown coloring may be even more beautiful. The offspring are "more gregarious" and "less elusive" than their more wary elders, Smyth observes, but young and old alike have powerful hind legs and are strong jumpers.

"These atoms of frogs leap enormous distances, never twice in the same direction," Dickerson observes. That trait makes them hard to catch, although their slender, delicate form, pointed head, and unusually alert appearance make them a pleasure to observe if chanced upon. (My son and I have always had better luck finding them early in the morning during the summer months.) The adult wood frog averages in size from about 1.25–3.75 inches or 30–94 mm (with legs nearly twice that length), and, with its distinguished eye mask, it really does cut a dashing figure.

"It not only looks much more intelligent," Dickerson once concluded, "but it is certainly less unintelligent . . . than other frogs."

Wood frog
This female wood frog, startled by the photographer during amplexus, has inflated her body and gone belly up in the water. Not to be deterred, the persistent male is attempting to crawl up on the female to fertilize more eggs.

American Toad
Bufo americanus

The image of a "toady"—a cringing, fawning sycophant who bows and scrapes to curry favor—owes a debt to the real toads of the world, but it is the toad's posture, not its personality, that is responsible.

The fat body, warty humped back, and short legs of *Bufo americanus*, the American toad, suggest a lowly or dirty creature to some, but, to others, its alleged ugliness is instead endearing. (Actually, the word "toady" derives from "toadeater," the name for a quack doctor's assistant who would eat "poisonous" toads to demonstrate the "potency" of quack medicines.)

The low-slung American toad may look a tad peculiar, but it is far from ugly. This toad comes dressed in a variety of colors, usually brown, gray, olive, or red, and it sports numerous red or yellowish warts and conspicuous dark-brown or black spots, the largest of which encircle only one or two warts (distinguishing this species from other toads). The mottled, earth-toned skin has a rough, almost horny appearance, and it provides excellent camouflage from enemies in the wild. Atop the toad's head are a pair of dazzling eyes with golden irises and gleaming black horizontal pupils.

The most common toad of the eastern United States, *Bufo americanus* can be found from New England south to northern Georgia, and across the Midwest from Minnesota southward to Mississippi. It prefers cool, damp habitats—from mountain forests to cultivated fields and household cellars—and spends its day in burrows it digs with its spurred hind feet or resting underneath logs, stones, sidewalks, or porches. Many a suburban backyard is host to this nocturnal species, which is celebrated by gardeners as a valiant ally.

The reason is simple: Toads have prodigious appetites and consume many of the gardener's worst enemies—slugs, hairy caterpillars, snails, cutworms, mosquitoes, locusts, grasshoppers, and other bugs. Barker recalls a 1936 publication called *Hand Book for the Curious* that included an inventory of the contents of a single toad's stomach on the morning after a night of hunting: "twenty-two large carpenter ants, two large-sized moth larvae, two sow bugs, five weevils, one flower beetle, one cricket, ten red ants, and five grasshoppers."

Some years earlier, a researcher calculated that 88 percent of the toad's diet consists of insects harmful to gardens and pastures. Based on this figure, Dickerson estimates, a toad will eat some 9,936 noxious insects over a period of three summer months—which explains why gardeners in France buy their own toads, and why a *Bufo* was featured prominently in 1994 on the cover of *Organic Gardening*.

The American toad's watchtower-like eyes, nimble front feet (which it uses like hands), and sticky tongue make this creature an efficient insect terminator. But, as is often the case, this hearty gardening partner is itself preyed upon by other animals—including hawks and owls, snakes, raccoons, skunks, and badgers. In a tight spot, the histrionic American toad will play dead, sprawling on its back, not moving a muscle for minutes at a time. (This ruse, however, doesn't always work.)

Far more effective is the toad's toxic defense system: large, kidney-shaped parotoid glands that secrete a white, acrid fluid that aggravates the mucous membranes of the mouth. Dogs, in particular, find an encounter with a toad extremely painful—the toxin can paralyze their respiratory system—and they rarely

American toads
To initiate amplexus, a female American toad will turn her back toward a male, encouraging him to clasp her body just behind the front legs. In his frenzy to mate, a male will grab another male by mistake—or sometimes a rock, dead fish, or leather boot.

American Toad
Bufo americanus

repeat their mistake. Humans should wash their hands after handling a toad and also avoid all contact with their eyes and mouth. (The one physical reaction to touching a toad that humans need not fear, of course, is coming down with warts, which are caused by a virus.)

During the 1960s, members of the drug culture in search of hallucinogenic thrills took to licking toads, despite the apparent risk from ingesting toxins; more recently, experimenters have sought psychedelic kicks by smoking dried toad venom.

"This looks like it could be a trend, and the toad is the one that will suffer," an official for the Arizona Department of Game and Fish told the *Wall Street Journal* in 1994. "Eventually, you'll probably see a much stiffer penalty for possession of a toad than for a controlled substance," a drug agent added. "The environmentalists have more clout than the cops."

Toad puffers aside, *Bufo americanus* and its relatives must beware hungry hognose snakes (fine herp actors themselves) and garter snakes, both of which will stalk and eat toads spurned by most other snakes.

"Such a queer snake one never saw," Dickerson once chuckled, after encountering a reptile with two long limbs sticking out of its jaws. It was, of course, a toad being swallowed headfirst—"too intent on his singing to see the stealthy approach of his enemy."

American toads
During the spring, American toads converge on ponds and streams in great writhing masses as they search for a mate. A gathering of toads is called a "knot"; a multitude of frogs is sometimes called a "congress."

Indeed, when a toad has procreation on its mind, its singlemindedness leaves it vulnerable to predation by its natural enemies and pulverization by nighttime traffic. And yet the intrepid toad will not abandon its quest for suitable aquatic breeding grounds and a willing mate. American toads emerge from their winter hibernation by March and immediately set out to find shallow ponds, creeks, or temporary pools of water. The male's spring advertisement call is a sweet, musical trill ("one of the most beautiful sounds in nature," Dickerson declares), emanating from a vocal sac inflated larger than the toad's head. Each male sings at a slightly different pitch, according to Lang Elliott, so a chorus of toads creates a considerable din.

Over the centuries, migrations of great numbers of male toads to their breeding sites, usually during or just after a rainstorm, have commenced so suddenly that observers have attributed the toads' sudden arrival to the rain itself, giving rise to popular folktales about toads raining from the sky. (In a few instances, however, amphibians have been transported some distance by tornadoes and hurricanes.)

Male toads are conspicuously "eager," which is to say they will clasp just about anything that moves (including a leather boot) or that looks the right size (rocks, other male toads, etc.). When one male is mounted by another, it issues a series of rapid squeaks or chirps—the release call—to alert the male on top of its mistake.

Female toads, so swollen with unfertilized eggs that they are much larger than their prospective mates, nudge a singing male before pairing. The male instantly embraces the female, clasping her with his swollen "nuptial thumbs" just behind her front legs. The female expresses some four

thousand to twelve thousand eggs in two long, transparent spiral tubes of jelly, which can reach lengths of up to 70 feet (21 meters). As the jellylike substance begins to swell, it becomes discolored by sediment in the water and soon resembles debris at the bottom. (Sometimes, however, the shallow water will dry up or be diverted before the eggs hatch; when this happens, the long strings of jelly are stranded on the rocks or shoreline vegetation and ultimately decompose.) Toad eggs hatch within three to ten days, and the tiny black tadpoles that emerge often remain together in "sibling schools," cruising the edges of the pond by day and dispersing at night.

Before their metamorphosis is complete, tadpoles prefer to climb partially or wholly out of the water; if confined to deep water, they "rush frantically to the top to exchange a bubble of foul air for one of fresh," Dickerson says, and eventually they drown.

Once established on land, the young toads shed their skin every few weeks (adults shed about four times a year). The molting takes only about five minutes, but it is fascinating to watch, as the toad draws its split skin into its mouth, using its front feet like hands, and eventually swallows the loosened skin in one piece.

In captivity, adult American toads may live to a ripe old age; one venerable toad was reliably reported to be thirty-six years old at the time of its death in an untimely accident.

Southern Toad
Bufo terrestris
The Southern toad, common throughout the southeastern United States from coastal Virginia south to Florida and west to Louisiana, is not only a frequent visitor to suburban lawns and gardens but

*D*uring the 1960s, members of the drug culture licked toads in search of hallucinogenic thrills; more recently, experimenters have sought psychedelic kicks by smoking dried toad venom.

Southern toad
The gentle-looking Southern toad burrows in sandy areas, fields, pine barrens, and hammocks during the heat of the day. Researchers have discovered that these toads have a well-developed homing instinct; when released a mile from their home breeding site, males will orient themselves and hop back, drawn by the trills of their companions.

Southern Toad
Bufo terrestris

several prominent knobs or crests.

"This toad is one of the meekest and gentlest looking creatures that ever lived a lowly life on the ground," Dickerson once declared. In captivity, the Southern toad will become tame and even accept food from a human hand, yet its timidity persists. When excited, the toad will twitch its toes nervously, usually as it eyes its prey.

When released near water, this toad may display a characteristic series of body movements. The toad "hops eagerly" towards the water and squats in the shallows, Dickerson writes. "After sitting quietly for a few moments, he turns around once or twice, then puts the water up on his eyes and the top of his head by means of his hands, using first one and then the other. . . . The wet feet are lifted one at a time, and their under surfaces are rubbed very dexterously over the toad's back and sides until all is wet."

The call of the Southern toad is a musical trill resembling that of the American toad, though shorter and higher in pitch (about a full octave higher, according to Conant and Collins). "Individuals may be freakish, hesitant, shrill, or even, rarely, open the mouth to scream, or with half-inflated throat give puzzling notes," Albert and Anna Wright record. "When many are calling close to the observer, the sound is deafening."

From February or March through September, Southern toads return to water—ponds, temporary pools, flooded meadows, or ditches—to seek mates and breed. Females lay long tube-like coils of jelly encasing 2,500–3,000 eggs, which hatch in about two to four days into tiny black tadpoles. The adult male's sense of hearing may be partly responsible for his skill at locating his home breeding site, according to Cochran; in field experi-

also a regular patron of convenience stores, patiently waiting outside at night for bugs attracted to the bright lights.

Southern toads (*Bufo terrestris*) are especially abundant in sandy areas, fields, pine barrens, and hammocks, where they burrow by day and emerge at night in search of food. The skin color of adults varies considerably, from shades of reddish or greenish brown to gray or black, with or without spots; younger toads are often a bright orange.

These are the toads of William Faulkner's *Light in August* and other works of southern literature—the amphibians which superstitious folk swear will cause warts when handled. The warts, however, belong exclusively to the toads, whose skin is covered with these rough (but nonviral) bumps and whose skull features

ments, many males collected and released over a mile away found their way home "drawn by the voices of their companions left in the pond"—a remarkable feat, she points out, for creatures averaging 2.50–4 inches (62–100 mm) in length "and having a hop of scarcely more than their own length."

The visual perceptions of Southern toads are apparently fairly acute as well. In experiments by Walter and Francis Kaess, toads demonstrated virtually no interest in a Lazy Susan laden with hamburger pellets when it was stationary, but once the motorized server began moving, the toads oriented themselves to the center of the revolving device and began "knocking off pellets of hamburger . . . like sharp-shooters in a shooting gallery." When placed on the spinning Lazy Susan alongside the beef, the toads also perceived the beef as a moving meal and gulped it down—perhaps deducing the meat was mobile, the authors surmised, because the background was in motion.

Fowler's Toad
Bufo woodhousii fowleri
Sometimes on warm evenings in the late spring or early summer, vacationers along the eastern seaboard step outside their cottages and are startled to hear the mournful sound of an infant crying in the darkness. The squalling continues at regular intervals, only to be answered by a woeful cry from another direction. Then the weirdly penetrating *waaaaaaaaah!* is joined by other voices, creating what sounds like a chorus of lost children . . . or a herd of bawling calves . . . or, more likely, an unholy choir of Fowler's toads.

Common along the sandy shorelines of lakes and coasts and in river valleys and pastures of the eastern and lower midwestern United States, the Fowler's toad

(*Bufo woodhousii fowleri*) performs such a striking serenade that American naturalists have long felt challenged to evoke the sound for others. Albert and Anna Wright compare the vocalization to the wail of a lamb; Stebbins characterizes the nasal *w-a-a-a-ah* as "an explosive wheeze" or "snore"; Elliott calls it a "buzzy, nasal trill"; and Dickerson states simply: "The quality is indescribable." But, she hastens to add, "others have compared it to the persistent whooping of a party of Indians."

The call is one characteristic that helps experts to distinguish the Fowler's toad from the American and the Southern toad. Other ways include counting the number of warts within each dark spot on the toad's back (there are invariably three or more warts) or studying the parotoid glands (they're never kidney-shaped in the Fowler's toad) that touch the ridges im-

*S*ometimes on warm evenings, vacationers along the American eastern seaboard are startled to hear what sounds like the mournful sound of an infant crying in the dark—then the weird *waaaaaaaaah!* is joined by other voices, an unholy choir of Fowler's toads.

Fowler's toad
The Fowler's toad is rarely as plump or squat as an American toad and is far more difficult to catch. A century ago, its mournful cry was compared to the sound of a band of whooping Indians.

Fowler's Toad
Bufo woodhousii fowleri

*T*he Colorado River toad reportedly can squirt its poison 12 feet (3.60 meters).

mediately behind the eyes. The skin coloration may help, too: Fowler's toads are typically dull brown or gray, or yellowish or greenish gray, while American toads more often sport a red or orange hue. The Fowler's toad also lacks spots on its underside.

Though named for the early Massachusetts naturalist S.P. Fowler, this toad also inherited a scientific name from another prominent naturalist, Samuel Washington Woodhouse, the southwestern surgeon/explorer for whom Woodhouse's toad is named. (Fowler's toad is an eastern subspecies.)

This toad is neither as squat nor as fat as the American toad, and it is considerably more agile, thus making it more difficult to catch. When handled roughly, however, it will roll over and play dead, even suspending its breathing movements until ready to right itself.

Fowler's toads begin their hibernation earlier and emerge several weeks later than American toads, as they apparently find it more difficult to endure the lower temperatures. (Sometimes they are even found hibernating in groups in chambers a foot or so below the ground.) They breed from mid-April to mid-August in ponds, lakes, lagoons, river margins, and roadside ditches.

"In regions where their presence is not even suspected," note Conant and Collins, "these toads may appear suddenly in large numbers when warm, heavy rains follow a long period of drought." Occasionally, Dickerson adds, there may be "so many hundreds of these toads that it would seem that all the Fowler's toads had assembled for miles around."

Females lay long, gelatinous strands, often tangled, of up to eight thousand eggs; arranged in one or two rows, these long strings lack the distinct inner parti-

tions characteristic of the American toad. Hybrids are not uncommon, since the range of the Fowler's toad overlaps that of other species. Hybrid offspring may evidence characteristics of both parents, according to Conant and Collins, and the calls of the male hybrids may be "difficult or impossible to identify."

Colorado River Toad
Bufo alvarius

The Colorado River toad (*Bufo alvarius*), more recently known as the Sonoran Desert toad, is impressive in sheer bulk alone. Measuring up to 7.50 inches (188 mm) in length, this species is regarded by the western amphibian expert Robert Stebbins as "the most spectacular toad of the West." In the United States, the Colorado River toad sometimes exceeds the length of the non-native cane toad, which has been known to reach 9.375 inches (234 mm) in some countries.

As its name suggests, the Colorado River toad is found along the (lower) Colorado River and also Arizona's Gila River, ranging into southwestern New Mexico and Sonora, Mexico, and across the southeastern border of California. Stebbins believes the toad is now near extinction in California, although some scientists concede that, despite man's destruction of the toad's natural habitat, the introduction of water to desert lands has actually helped the toad to survive. Thus, the toad's range has spread "since it discovered the benefits of irrigation and other man-made wet areas," Porter writes. In fact, he adds, "this toad can almost always be found beneath cattle troughs in otherwise dry locations."

(A collector who kept a Colorado River toad in a glass terrarium with a securely fastened lid returned home from work one day to find the toad sitting defiantly in her dog's water dish, having somehow managed to force the top off the tank to stage its escape.)

Unlike most toads, this species has a skin that is smooth and leathery (Dickerson calls it "rhinoceros-like"). In addition to long oval- or kidney-shaped parotoid glands, separated from the eye by prominent cranial crests, the Colorado River toad also has peculiar white warts at the corners of its mouth, as well as conspicuous large white glands on its legs. Secretions from the parotoids and other glands are extremely toxic, and dogs have been temporarily paralyzed or killed after seizing a toad in their jaws. In recent years, dried toxins from the Colorado River toad's glands have provided "toad smokers" in the United States with some mindbending hallucinogenic experiences.

Due to its impressive size and powerful toxins, this toad has few natural enemies besides man. However, if it perceives a threat, the toad will assume a butting pose and direct its parotoid glands toward the intruder. To counter the toad's defenses, raccoons have developed their own successful strategy for catching the animal: First, the raccoon pulls one toad after another from the spawning site, Hans Heusser says, then it "lays them on their back, pulls open the belly, and feeds on the insides without ever coming in contact with the skin."

Despite its rather formidable reputation (one author claims the "foot-long" Colorado River toad "squirts its poison 12 feet" or 3.60 meters), this toad is remarkably meek and gentle in voice and manner.

"When it is held in the hand," says Dickerson, "this toad jerks spasmodically,

Colorado River toad
Also known as the Sonoran Desert toad, this toad has unusual rhinoceros-like skin and a pair of large kidney-shaped parotoid glands situated behind the tympanum. The poison secreted by these glands can paralyze or kill a dog.

and vibrates the whole body, as if about to explode with wrath. The only sound, however, produced in protest is a gentle chirping note, less loud and emphatic than that of the American toad." (Albert and Anna Wright once caught three pairs and found the males "clucked like contented chickens.")

The weak, low-pitched voice of the male toad sounds like a ferryboat whistle, according to Stebbins; when large numbers assembled near water earlier in this century and advertised for mates, they apparently produced a deafening roar. Recent studies suggest that the toad's vocal abilities may have degenerated to the point where only a small percentage of males use their voices.

Colorado River Toad
Bufo alvarius

Cane toad

The cane toad, known for its voracious appetite, was introduced to Australia in the 1930s to control an infestation of beetles menacing the sugar cane crop. When the toads found cane fields lacked sufficient cover, however, they moved on and quickly overran the countryside. Today they pose a serious threat to Australia's native fauna, including frogs, reptiles, birds, and even small pets.

*F*emale cane toads lay thousands of eggs at a time; in one year, a single female may lay as many as thirty-five thousand eggs.

Cane Toad
Bufo marinus

The cane toad is truly a citizen of the world—but no one would have ever suspected as much as recently as sixty years ago. Prior to 1932, *Bufo marinus* (a.k.a. the cane, marine, neotropical, aga, or giant toad) was just a corpulent toad from French Guiana with an insatiable appetite for insect pests; introduced to the islands of Martinique and Barbados, and later to Jamaica and Puerto Rico, it made itself right at home and quickly ingratiated itself with local agricultural interests.

But then the troublesome toad was introduced to Hawaii and Australia, where, in short order, it opened up a Pandora's box of environmental and societal nightmares.

The history of this toad's introduction to Martinique, Barbados, and Ja-maica is somewhat sketchy, Australian frog authority Michael J. Tyler reports, though apparently the large toads were brought in to control insect and rodent pests. In 1920, however, a chain of events was set into motion by an agronomist in Puerto Rico that was to have worldwide consequences. Twelve toads were imported from Barbados or Trinidad and released at an agricultural experimental station (joined a few years later by forty more) to control an infestation of beetles that threatened the banana, coconut, breadfruit, and sugar cane crops. At that time, Tyler says, there were "no known control measures" against the beetles, and plantation owners were even paying a bounty on every beetle that was rounded up.

"Faced with a potential crisis situation, the cane toad was viewed as the answer to plantation owners' prayers," Tyler explains. "Here was an animal that bred like rabbits, required no maintenance, and, without question, would devour every insect it encountered. Not only was it more efficient than human collectors, but it was free!"

When the International Sugar Cane Technologists Convention was held in Puerto Rico in March 1932, the cane toad's impact on the host country's economy was highly touted; "overnight," Tyler reports, "the cane toad became almost sacred."

One month later, a Hawaiian sugar planter collected 154 cane toads in Puerto Rico and packed them into four crates—three of which he sent back to Hawaii by steamer, the fourth by airplane. Of the original 154 toads, 148 or 149 survived their journeys, and within seventeen months they had increased their numbers dramatically (some would say "opportunistically") to an astonishing 105,517. Shortly thereafter, some of these toads were bidding Hawaii "aloha" and were headed for new territories to conquer in the South Pacific.

In 1935, a sugar cane researcher collected 102 Hawaiian cane toads and sent them to Queensland for study. After one particularly fruitful breeding season, some 3,400 young toads were "liberated" on the Australian continent in an experimental effort to control the grayback cane beetle.

Australia has never been the same since.

Today, millions of voracious cane toads can be found in Queensland and New South Wales, and they periodically threaten to invade other states as well. In fact, they are so abundant in some areas, Halliday and Adler report, that "nighttime gardens become a slowly moving

Cane Toad
Bufo marinus

dark-shuffling sea of toads, and in the morning roads are littered with squashed bodies run over in the night." Motorists unlucky enough to encounter these creatures crossing highways in search of breeding pools vividly recall the *pop, pop, pop* sound of cane toads crunching beneath their tires.

These giant toads, Australians quickly discovered, eat as many creatures "beneficial to agriculture" as pests, according to Halliday and Adler. In Queensland, the toads began devouring local populations of frogs and snakes, menaced Brisbane's honey industry, and had a negative impact on birds such as the ibis, which "were killed off when they tried to eat the toad, either by being poisoned or by having the toad impacted in the throat," Maurice and Robert Burton report.

Because this behemoth *Bufo* found human habitation to its liking, it invaded local gardens, parks, fields, fish ponds, canals, and water tanks, where it reproduced exponentially. Mortified by the sudden appearance of these huge toads and upset that their pets were intimidated (some toads hopped up on doorsteps and acquired a taste for dog and cat food), Australians formed groups called "Toad Busters" and set out at night wielding

A hormonelike substance called serotonin found in the cane toad causes blood vessels to contract; it is being studied by scientists, who believe it may aid treatment of human heart disease, cancer, mental illness, and allergies.

nets, cricket bats, and American baseball bats to collect bounties or to engage in gleeful rounds of toad bashing. In due time, a movie by Mark Lewis called *Cane Toads: An Unnatural History* (characterized as a cross between a "National Geographic Special" and a Monty Python sketch) became a cult film at home and abroad.

Today, the infamous cane toad has spread, via deliberate or accidental human introduction, throughout South America, Central America, Mexico, and into southeast Texas and parts of Florida, as well as the Caribbean, Hawaii, Taiwan, the Philippines, New Guinea, Fiji, Australia, and elsewhere. Presumed to be the world's largest toad, it can grow up to 10 inches or 250 mm in length—although it rarely tops 7 inches or 175 mm in the United States—and can weigh as much as 3 pounds (1.35 kg). The cane toad has a warty skin and is generally a mottled brown in appearance, or some color variation of red, yellow, green, or black.

It sports a pair of enormous parotoid glands, widely feared for their toxicity. These triangular glands secrete a milky-white venom that induces nausea or vomiting and can paralyze or kill a dog; in Hawaii, as many as fifty canine deaths are attributed to cane toads each year. People, too, can suffer at the glands of these toads, and humans have reportedly died after confusing cane toads with edible species of frogs or after mistaking cane toad eggs for varieties of other caviar-like frogs' eggs.

Females lay thousands of eggs at a time, sometimes reportedly in slightly brackish bodies of water (hence the name "marine toad"); in one year, a single female was said to have laid as many as thirty-five thousand eggs. The call of the male is described variously as a loud snoring bark, a booming trill, a tremulous bass, a mechanical popping, or the sound of a distant tractor.

When alarmed, the cane toad elevates its rear end and points its massive parotoid glands toward the intruder, sometimes squirting its toxins or spraying urine considerable distances. A hormone-like substance called serotonin found in the toad's glandular secretions is currently being studied by scientists, who believe its role in causing blood vessels to contract may lead to significant medical breakthroughs in treating human heart disease, cancer, mental illness, and allergies.

European Green Toad
Bufo viridis

Perhaps the secret of the great German violinists of the eighteenth and nineteenth centuries can be explained by something as unlikely as . . . a toad. When the musicians' fingers grew moist, it seems, they would check the perspiration by rubbing their hands across the back of *Bufo viridis*, the European green toad. The toad's copious skin secretions had the aroma of a linseed poultice and may have had a soothing or softening effect.

Whether the European green toad contributed significantly to the classical nocturnes and symphonies performed in the salons and concert halls of Europe may never be known, but this species remains one of the most common toads in central and southern Europe and, because of its vivid olive and emerald-green spots, perhaps its most beautiful.

The colorful patches of green adorn a highly variable cream, gray, or brownish green back, often flecked with specks of vermilion. On some individuals, a yellow vertebral stripe runs down the back between the well-developed parotoid glands. The toad's iris is the color of brass, with very fine dark dots.

The green toad ranges throughout

Europe (excluding the British Isles, France, and the Iberian peninsula), south to the Mediterranean islands and North Africa, and east through Russia, western and central Asia to the Himalayas, where specimens have been found at record altitudes of 15,000 feet (4,500 meters).

These medium-sized toads (2.75–4 inches or 69–100 mm) are mostly nocturnal, emerging at dusk to stalk their insect prey; younger specimens can be seen by day during the summer, hopping down back alleys in small villages and suburbs. In Germany, these toads are so common around human habitation that they are called *Hausunken*, or "house toads," congregating in cellars where they seek out moisture. In recent years, widespread industrial pollution of the Rhine and other rivers has had a serious impact on the toad populations of Europe. Near Stuttgart, for example, researchers have found that as many as 35–55 percent of green toad tadpoles exhibit abnormalities from radioactive pollution (similar to abnormalities studied at the University of Hiroshima in Japan).

During the breeding season, green toads leave their daytime holes in open lowlands, gardens, orchards, and other locations (including rubbish heaps and waste dumps) to mate in ponds or roadside ditches. Curiously, this amphibian is one of only a very few able to spawn in brackish water—in this case, in steppe regions where salt water may be the only water available. Male green toads clasp their mate under the arms and sometimes hold the embrace for several days until the female has laid between five thousand and thirteen thousand eggs. Due to the overlap of ranges with other species, the green toad occasionally hybridizes with its fellow European toads.

The call of the European green toad

European green toad
The European green toad's beautiful olive-green coloration is adorned with emerald-green spots and flecks of red. This toad is one of only a few amphibians found in salty, brackish water, where it sometimes spawns.

has been likened to the sound of crickets, the noise of a spinning top, and the creak of a door, but, according to George Boulenger, the "clear, sonorous" tone actually brings to mind a London policeman's whistle.

In his classic study of tailless amphibians of Europe, Boulenger recounts a story about the effect of a European green toad's poison on a small terrier that accompanied a professor on a collecting expedition. The toad, discovered beneath a stone, was attacked by the dog, Boulenger wrote, "but no sooner seized was let go again with signs of great repulsion; the toad had instantly become covered with a thick white secretion. The dog approached it once more and then withdrew, sneezing and howling and rubbing its foaming mouth on the grass." A few minutes later, the dog was "seized with convulsions and had to be carried home exhausted. On the next day it had a swollen mouth and burning nose. It did not recover until the following day."

German violinists of the eighteenth and nineteenth centuries rubbed their hands across the backs of European green toads to halt perspiration.

African red toad
The skin of the African red toad is not dry or granular like that of most toads. The male of this species has a deep, booming voice and often calls while floating in a pond, one forefoot clinging to a reed.

The red toad deposits jellylike strands of up to twenty thousand eggs; each strand is roughly 4 feet (1.20 meters) in length.

African Red Toad
Bufo carens

The African red toad (*Bufo carens*) is found in open or bushy savannas from the Republic of South Africa north to Kenya. By day it remains hidden, but it announces its presence at night with a deep, muffled boom. This call is a long, drawn-out *ooomp* or *urrrmp*, South African frog expert Vincent Wager reports, usually issued while the toad is floating in a waterhole or stream or clasping a reed with a single hand or foot.

The red toad, which averages about 3.50 inches (88 mm) in length, is indeed red or reddish brown in color, with darker cryptic patterns that provide camouflage. Oddly enough, this toad lacks parotoid glands, although it does have pronounced ridges that run from its eyes to just behind its front legs. ("Other peculiar skeletal, biochemical, and developmental features," Tandy and Keith point out, "make uncertain its placement in the genus *Bufo*.")

During the day, the African red toad prefers to remain out of sight in holes, under logs, or among dead leaves; at night, it is often seen in the vicinity of outdoor lights, where it feeds on insects attracted to the illumination.

At the onset of the rainy season, the red toad breeds in shallow water, depositing jelly strands of up to twenty thousand eggs along the shore in parallel rows, each roughly 4 feet (1.20 meters) long, entwined around vegetation or rocks.

Eastern Spadefoot Toad
Scaphiopus holbrookii holbrookii

Hurricanes are always an "interesting" event to herpetologists, a Florida naturalist once pointed out, because the torrential rains whip up intense activity among reptiles and amphibians—especially the Eastern spadefoot toad (*Scaphiopus holbrookii holbrookii*), an explosive breeder that emerges from its underground burrow as if on cue during periods of heavy rain. This peculiar pop-eyed toad, which has a smooth, frog-like skin and horny spades on its hind feet, is one of six North American spadefoots, but it is the only species found east of the Mississippi River.

After a downpour has begun, the first male spadefoot to reach a suitable stand of water sounds his clarion call, summoning more and more toads (sometimes by the hundreds or thousands) until the night reverberates with explosive grunts and plaintive groans that sound just like the cawing of immature crows. Or, some say, like the hectoring sounds of a cross baby, or the nasal *waank-waank* of a rookery of young herons, or the surging *errrrah!* of a person vomiting.

However one characterizes the advertisement cry of the spadefoot (which, when performed in a chorus, can make "as

much noise as a steam calliope," Albert and Anna Wright attest), the ensuing racket is music to the ears of nearby females, which descend upon the breeding sites before they dry up and swim out to the amorous males.

Males grab out to available spadefoots of either sex, sometimes intruding upon a mating pair and creating what Williams and Carmichael call "a rather frenzied *menage a trois*"; after mating, the female lays strings of eggs that can hatch in just two days or less. The little bronze or brown tadpoles that emerge cluster together "in a dense mass like a swarm of bees," Olive Goin observes, beating the water to a froth in "a last desperate effort to achieve toadhood" before the water evaporates.

Because the food supply in temporary pools is limited—especially in desert or semi-desert areas of the western and

Eastern spadefoot toads
The fascinating "pop eyes" of the Eastern spadefoot toad have a unique jewel-like or metallic quality. The irises of these three spadefoot toads range from copper to greenish gold and turquoise.

Eastern spadefoot toad

An albino Eastern spadefoot toad lacks the pigmentation that gives this species its characteristic brown, gray, or greenish yellow skin color. Using shovel-like spades on its hind legs, a spadefoot toad can quickly bury itself in the soil, wriggling its hips, an observer once remarked, like "the contortions of a plump hula dancer."

Eastern Spadefoot Toad
Scaphiopus holbrookii holbrookii

southwestern United States, where the other five species of spadefoots live—the tadpoles sometimes resort to cannibalism. While this practice may sound savage to some, Arthur Bragg says in his spadefoot toad tome, *Gnomes of the Night*, "if every spadefoot egg laid should result in an adult spadefoot, there would soon be no room on the face of the earth for anything else."

The surviving tadpoles often leave the water well before their tails have disappeared (if they stay in the water too long, they will drown) and scurry across the ground on their short legs in search of small insects.

The adult Eastern spadefoot—also known as the storm toad or hermit spadefoot—is usually brown, dark green, or gray, with a conspicuous pair of yellow lines down the back that creates a lyre or hourglass design. The toad's prominent round pop eyes are a brilliant gold color, with rare vertical pupils; its skin is soft, moist, and relatively smooth. Secretions from the skin glands have a musty odor that reminds people of garlic (the German name for a European spadefoot is *Knoblauchskrote*, or "garlic toad") and also "one of the nastiest tastes of which I am aware," Bragg reports. Persons who handle these toads often develop a strong allergic reaction, according to Conant and Collins, including violent sneezing and watery eyes.

The Eastern spadefoot grows up to 2.875 inches (72 mm) long, not including the well-developed hind legs and hardened sickle-shaped spade on each heel. These horny spades permit the toad to dig backwards into sandy or loose soil, wriggling its hips sidewise, Goin observes, in "the contortions of a plump hula dancer."

These solitary toads can easily burrow down several feet; Dickerson recalls that a gravedigger once discovered a spadefoot some 3 feet (0.90 meters) below the surface of the ground, and Bragg cites a case where a spadefoot was found buried 15 feet (4.50 meters).

These toads can remain underground for weeks, perhaps months, at a time, although their nocturnal forays aboveground for food are rarely witnessed by humans. Scientists have discovered that the Eastern spadefoot has a well-developed "homing" instinct, returning night after night to the same burrow and shoveling open the entrance if it has been covered up. During drought, Eastern spadefoots and their desert relatives "excrete a fluid, curl into a tight ball, and lie dormant," Tyning reports. The dirt surrounding the toad is hardened by the secretion, sealing the chamber and retaining whatever moisture is available. These burrows are remarkably effective, as spadefoots have been found alive amid the ashes of a smoldering brush fire.

These stout, "uncanny-looking" toads strike Dickerson as somewhat "unintelligent" creatures, but Bragg has demonstrated that young plains spadefoots can learn by trial and error, repeatedly rejecting an offensive species of ant after just one unpleasant encounter.

By day, the secretive spadefoot crouches in its burrow, drawing its legs up under its body and resting its chin on its front feet or poking its snout and eyes through the soil to observe its surroundings. But come a heavy rainstorm or prolonged drizzle (at temperatures above 52 degrees F or 11 degrees C), the toad will re-emerge to initiate its curiously spasmodic breeding activity.

Oriental Fire-Bellied Toad
Bombina orientalis

The Oriental fire-bellied toad (*Bombina orientalis*), a native of Korea, northeastern China, and southeastern Russia, is one of four or five Asian and European fire-bellied toads celebrated for the fiery red, orange, or yellow "flash colors" visible on their undersides. Dotted with black spots, these colorful bellies are displayed when the toad assumes its characteristic defensive position—arching its back and rising up on its legs to warn predators to back off.

For good reason. The Oriental fire-bellied toad and its relatives, including the yellow-bellied or variegated toad (*Bombina variegata*) of central and southern Europe

and the "unke" fire-bellied toad (*Bombina bombina*) of central and eastern Europe, secrete a distasteful toxin that deters most enemies. This skin secretion is a foamy white fluid, caustic and irritating, which reeks of an odor likened to the smell of leeks. Herpetologists who handle these toads say the vapor causes them to sneeze and experience runny eyes.

Despite the potency of its poison, a fire-bellied toad will instinctively dive to the bottom of the body of water it is swimming in if frightened; if alarmed while on land, however, it strikes a pose called the "canoe position." Pushing its head up and arching its back, the toad covers its eyes with its hands ("as if it cannot bear to look at its tormentor," Maurice and Robert

Oriental fire-bellied toad
The Oriental fire-bellied toad's warty green or brown body, scattered with glossy black spots, is difficult to see from above in ponds and rice paddies. When disturbed, its first response is to dive to the bottom and bury itself in the mud; if forced to confront its tormentor, however, it may instinctively cover its eyes with its forefeet.

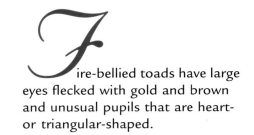

Fire-bellied toads have large eyes flecked with gold and brown and unusual pupils that are heart- or triangular-shaped.

Oriental fire-bellied toad
The underside of the Oriental fire-bellied toad displays prominent red or orange warning colors, marbled with dark spots, to alert predators to its highly toxic skin secretions. Generations of fire-bellied toads bred in captivity sometimes exhibit yellow undersides.

Oriental Fire-Bellied Toad
Bombina orientalis

regions. Fire-bellies frequently live together in social groups, sunning themselves on land near their home waters or drifting on the water's surface with their legs splayed in different directions. They thrive on insects, worms, and snails, but their peculiar rounded tongues are unable to shoot out and snatch prey like the tongues of most other frogs.

The call of the fire-bellied toad is loud but rather melodious, described by some as a honking call and by others as a musical bell-like ringing. (Massimo Capula, on the other hand, calls it a "mournful, nasal croak.") In Germany, *B. bombina* is sometimes called "Unke"—the common word for "toad" but also an apparent reference to its piercing *unk-unk* advertisement call. The eggs of female fire-bellied toads are fertilized one by one and laid under stones or attached to vegetation or other debris.

Surinam Toad
Pipa pipa

The physical shape of the Surinam toad invites some pretty offbeat comparisons: This aquatic animal "could easily be mistaken for a flat square mud pie with two beady eyes," asserts one observer; herpetologist Doris Cochran expands: "It is shaped like a squarish pancake—a somewhat scorched pancake at that."

Found in the muddy, often polluted standing waters and rivers of tropical South America—from Trinidad, Surinam, and Guyana southward through Brazil, Bolivia, and Peru—the drab-looking Surinam toad (*Pipa pipa*) has inspired scientific consternation and debate for nearly three centuries, not because of its peculiar body shape but because of its bizarre breeding and brooding habits.

In 1705, the first published account of the Surinam toad's incubation period claimed that the baby toads grew directly

Burton suggest) and positions its webbed hind feet along the sides of its body.

Fire-bellied toads grow to about 1.25–2 inches (31–50 mm) in length (*Bombina maxima* of southern China and eastern Siberia grows to 3 inches or 75 mm). The colors on their backs range from bright green or dull gray to blue-black, depending on the species, marbled with dark spots and small knobby protrusions or tubercles. The large eyes are flecked with gold and brown, and the unusual pupils are heart- or triangular-shaped.

Active both by day and by night, these toads live near ponds, lakes, streams, quarries, ditches, rice paddies, or other sources of water; some species are almost exclusively aquatic. The variegated fire-bellied toad and several others are found at higher altitudes in hilly or mountainous

out of the mother's back—a phenomenon well recognized but never adequately explained. In 1710, a Dutch anatomist concluded that the "honeycomb pockets" on the female's back had absolutely no connection at all with the "maternal tissues"; five years later, a scientist insisted that the babies were carried by the male, not the female. Then in 1765, a herpetologist at the London Zoo reported that females deposited their eggs in the sand; males then scooped them up, positioned the eggs on the mother's back, and fertilized them.

Other accounts followed, until persuasive photographs and movies taken by George and Mary Rabb at Chicago's Brookfield Zoo established that the pairs flip themselves over, and—in a single second, at the peak of their somersault—the female lays three to ten eggs that descend onto the male's belly. One half-flip later, the male fertilizes the eggs, presses them into the spongy, pillow-like skin of the female's back, and is ready to repeat the cycle. After approximately sixty eggs are distributed across the female's back, her skin swells up and encapsulates the eggs until fully formed toadlets emerge two to four months later.

This tricky two-part somersault seems quite an achievement for a lower anuran (Duellman calls the feat "a truly graceful display of underwater acrobatics"), and it accounts for the species' longstanding popularity among aquarium hobbyists. On the other hand, the toad itself is not at all handsome: Its skin color is dark gray or brownish black, providing ideal camouflage for the tongueless scavenger as it rakes the muddy river bottom with long, starlike filaments on the tips of its fingers.

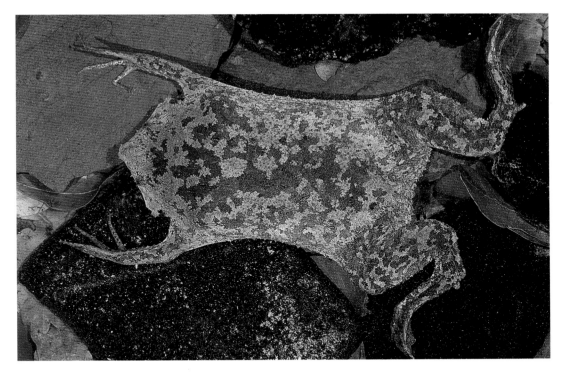

Surinam toad
The drab coloration of the Surinam toad provides camouflage in the muddy waters of South American rivers and streams. This peculiar-looking species has a pancake-shaped body, flat head, and beady, lidless eyes.

The Surinam toad's lidless black eyes, located near the front of its flat, triangular-shaped head, are quite small, yet they afford the animal an ample range of vision with which to glimpse enemies. Averaging 4–8 inches (100–200 mm) in length, these sluggish-looking toads rest on the bottom of the Amazon and Orinoco River basins by day, becoming active by night when they probe for invertebrates with the sensitive appendages on their fingertips. In captivity, their mating call is a rapid metallic *click-click-click*—unique among frogs, Smyth points out, because it is produced not by air vibrating the vocal cords but by the "cracking" of disks on two bones when the bones are moved.

Surinam Toad
Pipa pipa

103

African Clawed Frog
Xenopus laevis

African Clawed Frog
Xenopus laevis

African clawed frog
Whereas the African clawed frog typically has olive-brown or gray skin, usually mottled with dark blotches, albino specimens are common. They are often sold in pet shops as a novelty item for freshwater fish tanks.

"Just when you thought it was safe to go back into the water," California wildlife officials warned in the 1970s (borrowing a tag line from the *Jaws* movies), along came a new underwater threat to the citizenry of the state: the African clawed frog. The name sounded sinister enough—"claws" and "jaws" both suggesting an element of peril—but the frog was a relatively puny 2–5.625 inches (50–141 mm), nowhere near the size of a great white shark. As it turned out, the real victims were the state's natural residents—the fish, frogs, and other wildlife inhabiting California's streams and ponds that fell prey to this carnivorous clawed frog (*Xenopus laevis*) and its insatiable appetite.

Today, four states prohibit importation and possession of the African clawed frog—California, Arizona, Nevada, and Utah—but this aquatic species remains popular elsewhere as an aquarium pet, and black-market trade continues in the West and Southwest.

The African clawed frog hasn't always been regarded as a pariah; in fact, it once played a significant international role in the development and refinement of pregnancy testing. In the late 1920s, scientists discovered that laboratory mice injected with urine from pregnant women underwent changes in their ovaries. The mice had to be killed, however, and the test results, though highly reliable, were not available for five days. Within a year, it was found that rabbits could be substituted for mice, and the time span was reduced to one or two days. Then, in 1931, scientists in Cape Town, South Africa, discovered that injections of urine from pregnant women would induce the discharge of eggs from unmated female clawed frogs.

"Here was a test that was not only twice as quick as any other"—five to eighteen hours—"but it left the animal alive," Halliday and Adler recount. Although there were rival claimants to the discovery and simultaneous experimental findings in South Africa and London, the ultimate result was a tremendous demand for African clawed frogs all over the world. Later it was found that injections into male clawed frogs would also trigger a reaction (release of sperm), and eventually scientists determined that frogs of almost any species were suitable. On rare occasions, the frog-based tests produced unexpected results, as was the case with a Chicago woman who ate spicy food at a Mexican restaurant the evening before her test. The following day, Heusser relates, her urine sample killed all the frogs. Today, doctors' standard pregnancy tests have a 98 percent accuracy rate, compared with the earlier 87 percent correct-diagnosis rate with *Xenopus*.

The African clawed frog is truly an odd-looking creature, its appearance suggesting a frog flattened by a hit-and-run driver. Its relatively weak front legs have long, slender fingers (a South American variety has starlike projections on its front toes), useful for catching prey or fanning food toward the mouth, while the powerful hind legs have webbed inner toes and black curved claws that can rake up mud to uncover food and stir up silt to distract an enemy. Claws, in fact, are quite unusual on frogs, which explains adoption of the Greek word *Xenopus* ("peculiar foot") for the scientific name.

In Port Elizabeth, South Africa, colonists had their own name for this frog: "plathander" (or "platanna" or "platie"), meaning "flat hands." Found in local rivers, veldt ponds, and reservoirs, these frogs are easily recognized by their peculiar limbs, the tiny eyes with round pupils on the top of their heads, and smooth, slippery skin. The olive-brown or gray skin, usually mottled with dark blotches, is sometimes slimy and can give off a musky odor that may repel predators. Albino specimens are common and sold in pet shops as a novelty item for freshwater fish tanks.

Originally, the ubiquitous clawed frogs of South Africa were presumed to be strictly aquatic—until, that is, they began turning up in rain puddles throughout central, eastern and southern Africa. This suggested they could also maneuver on land.

It cannot survive for long out of water, *Xenopus* authority Elizabeth Deuchar reports, but, if required to cross land, "it is capable of moving reasonably fast by a series of lolloping leaps, landing flat on its belly each time and slithering off course if the surface is too smooth."

In water, however, African clawed frogs are extremely proficient swimmers, using their front legs as paddles and kicking with their strong hind legs. When encountering enemies, they even demonstrate a remarkable ability to swim or jump backwards. (Describing their underwater movements, Cochran says these frogs have "the strength and certainty of a small submarine.") During the dry season, when water holes and streams dry up temporarily, the frogs dig down deep into the mud and estivate until the onset of rains and flooding.

With these rains come new sources of food, and the involuntarily slimmed-down estivaters emerge to indulge their aggressive and competitive feeding habits (and well-recognized cannibalism). One benefit to humanity of the frog's voracious appetite is the impact on local mosquito populations: African clawed

African clawed frog
The African clawed frog has large webbed feet equipped with sharp claws on the inner toes. Introduced to California from South Africa by researchers and pet hobbyists, this frog breeds like a rabbit and eats just about anything it can get into its mouth, posing a serious threat to native wildlife.

frogs eat great quantities of mosquito eggs and larvae and have helped to control or reduce the incidence of malaria in a number of countries.

As breeders go, clawed frogs are rather prolific (and, in captivity, are often observed in "amorous embrace, regardless of the season," Gadow reports). The males call from underwater, croaking a curious *tick-tick-tick* by day and night that sounds "rather like a squeaky water-tap being turned on," according to Deuchar. Males grasp their mates by the loins in a pelvic amplexus position, and females produce up to two thousand eggs, usually attaching them to the stems of water plants. The eggs hatch within about thirty-six hours, and the tiny tadpoles (which sport catfish-like whiskers called barbels) congregate head down in deep water, Cochran observes, sucking protozoa into their mouths rather than scraping algae like most other species.

The African clawed frog once played an important role in pregnancy testing: In 1931, South African scientists discovered that injections of urine from pregnant women induced the discharge of eggs from unmated female clawed frogs.

*B*atrachotoxins secreted by dart-poison frogs may prove valuable for medical science, particularly the study of anesthetics, muscle relaxants, cardiac stimulants, and control of fibrillation (rapid or irregular heartbeat).

The so-called dwarf African clawed frog (*Hymenochirus curtipes*) is a native of rain forests of equatorial West Africa. A member of the same genus as the African clawed frog but belonging to a different family, it seems to be intermediate species between *Xenopus* and the Surinam toad. First identified in the lower Congo basin in 1896, these small (1–1.50 inches, or 25–38 mm, long) gray-brown aquatic frogs spawn on their backs on the water's surface, like the Surinam toad, but leave their eggs to float or sink to the bottom of the pond.

Dart-Poison Frogs

Some of the most beautiful frogs in the world are so new to science they don't even have names yet—popular or scientific. Even their collective designation—as "dart-poison frogs," "poison-dart frogs," or "poison-arrow frogs"—has fluctuated over the past two decades, although herpetologists now seem to favor "dart-poison frogs."

By whatever name, these 135-plus species (estimates vary considerably) from the rain forests of Central and South America sport a range of bold colors, from hot yellow and strawberry red to deep blue, purple, and green. Some are patterned with dark stripes or swirls; others have spots or flecks; still others are a solid color. Yet, even within a single species, the color patterns vary widely.

Although almost all species of frogs and toads harbor at least a trace of poison in their glands, they generally rely on inconspicuous skin coloring (and speed) for survival. Dominant shades of green, brown, and gray offer camouflage for frogs glimpsed from above, and mottled yellow or white undersides suggest light overhead to underwater predators.

The bright colors and contrasting bands of dart-poison frogs, on the other hand, are a bold advertisement of the frogs' presence. Like the vivid hues of certain poisonous snakes and butterflies, these colors serve as a natural warning label for enemies. (Apparently a few enemies, including certain snakes, are immune to the poisons, as are the frogs themselves, although some specimens subjected to stress in captivity may have died from their own lethal secretions.) On other species, this palette of dazzling skin colors would serve little purpose, since most frogs are active at night; dart-poison frogs, on the other hand, are active during the day, when their colors attract maximum attention.

"The little frog hops about in the daytime, dressed in a bright livery of red and blue," one nineteenth-century naturalist wrote. "He cannot be mistaken for any other, and his flaming vest and blue stockings show that he does not court concealment."

The outside world first learned of the existence of these poisonous frogs from a British naval captain, Charles Stuart Cochrane, who published an account of his travels in Colombia during the 1820s. While crossing the Andes, Cochrane encountered native Indians who collected yellow-and-black frogs, confined them in hollow canes, and kept them alive until they were needed for hunting.

"They take one of the unfortunate reptiles," Cochrane wrote, "and pass a pointed piece of wood down his throat, and out one of his legs. The torture makes the poor frog perspire very much, especially on the back, which becomes covered with white froth."

The natives then dipped or rolled the tips of their arrows in the froth, which retained its potency for up to an entire year. A yellow oil that appeared beneath

*J*n the 1820s, British naval captain Charles Stuart Cochrane first told the world of the Colombian Indians' use of the toxic skin secretions of the dart-poison frogs on the tips of their hunting arrows.

Dart-poison frog
Scientists have difficulty identifying many dart-poison frogs because their colors vary so widely, even among members of the same species. In its "bull's-eye" phase, Dendrobates histrionicus *sports bright orange circles on dark brown skin.*

Dart-Poison Frogs
Dendrobates and *Phyllobates*

Dart-poison frog
Phyllobates bicolor *is one of the most toxic of all dart-poison frogs. This ground-dwelling species lives in the Pacific river area of western Colombia, where the Choco Indians reportedly still dip blow-pipe arrows in the frog's lethal skin secretions.*

the white froth was also scraped off, Cochrane observed; this oil "retains its deadly influence for four or six months, according to the goodness (as they say) of the frog. By this means, from one frog sufficient poison is obtained for about fifty arrows."

Highly effective for hunting jaguars, monkeys, birds, and small game, or for waging war against human enemies, this poison could also be obtained by roasting frogs over a fire; the glands would then "sweat" drops of poison, which could be collected and stored in containers. Today, according to Charles W. Myers of the American Museum of Natural History and John W. Daly of the National Institutes of Health, dart-poison frogs are no longer used for poisoning arrows, and a decline in the use of blowguns has reduced dependence on animal poisons.

Nonetheless, these toxins are of great interest to medical researchers because of their remarkable potency (German herpetologist Ralf Heselhaus calls dart-poison frogs "the Borgias of the amphibians"). Scientists believe that secretions from the golden-yellow *Phyllobates bicolor*, for example, are so toxic that 0.0000004 oz. (0.0000112 grams) may be enough to kill a person. Myers and Daly recall an incident when, after handling some frogs, they burned all the rubber gloves they had worn; the next day, however, they discovered a dog and some chickens lying dead near their "contaminated" garbage after a rainstorm extinguished the trash fire—victims, they concluded, of the poison.

Frog toxins work quickly, attacking the nerves and muscles. Nerve cells "can no longer transmit impulses," Myers and Daly report, "and muscle cells remain in an activated, contracted state." The result is death by respiratory or muscular paralysis. Batrachotoxins secreted by these frogs

may prove especially valuable for medical science and the study of anesthetics, muscle relaxants, cardiac stimulants, and control of fibrillation (rapid or irregular heartbeat).

At the National Aquarium in Baltimore, Maryland, where one of the most spellbinding exhibits of live dart-poison frogs in the United States is currently housed, herpetologists have had success breeding as many as twenty species, but they have also encountered a potential stumbling block for medical researchers: Frogs born in captivity apparently do not secrete toxins. Scientists aren't sure why, but they speculate that the absence of certain bacteria or perhaps something missing from the diet in captivity may be the reason.

Visitors to the National Aquarium sometimes hear the frogs' distinctive peeps, chirps, and trills, which advertise the availability of males to females and also define territory. Males (and some females) often behave aggressively toward other males, engaging in ritualized wrestling bouts with one another on their hind legs.

Unlike males of most frog species, which are smaller than females, male dart-poison frogs are generally about the same size as females; during amplexus, the male has to clasp his mate under her chin, instead of around her waist, while engaging in external fertilization of eggs. Clutches of eggs are quite small (rarely exceeding forty eggs), and the eggs are often kept moist and protected by a parent. Females deposit their eggs on land in dampness beneath leaf litter, but, after the tadpoles emerge, water is required for their development. At this point, the attending parent squats in the gelatinous mass "right among the larvae," Heselhaus notes, which "respond to the sensations of

Strawberry dart-poison frog
The strawberry dart-poison frog, Dendrobates pumilio, *lives in lowland forests of Nicaragua, Costa Rica, and Panama. Although these frogs are usually bright strawberry-red or orange, with black dots on the back and blue or black legs, widespread variations occur, from chocolate-brown to blue and olive-green.*

Dart-poison frog
The dart-poison frog Dendrobates auratus *sports an astonishing range of fifteen color variations, including green bands on black and yellow-gold stripes on brown. These shy frogs from Central and South America are often found on cocoa plantations, where rotting fruit attracts swarms of tiny insects.*

movement and wriggle up the father's legs" onto his back. The parent then deposits its young in a water-filled bromeliad or pool of water. After the young frogs develop, they return to their natural habitat—arboreal or terrestrial—where they seek out a diet of ants, termites, and other insects.

Of the scores of species in the family Dendrobatidae (authority Jerry Walls calculates in a new book that there are about 170), the strawberry dart-poison frog (*Dendrobates pumilio*) is one of the best

known, familiar from its many appearances on T-shirts, magazine covers, and notecards. Although named for the intense metallic-red skin of Costa Rican specimens, in Panama these tiny frogs sport a bewildering array of other colors, including orange, green, and blue. The male's call is a loud *app-app-app*, which observers say causes the frog's entire body to vibrate.

The blue dart-poison frog (*Dendrobates azureus*), found exclusively in the jungles and savannas of the Republic of

*T*he "rocket frogs" (*Colostethus*) of Central and South America grow to only about 0.625 inches (17 mm long) and zip about as fast as rockets.

Dart-poison frogs

Two color morphs of the dart-poison frog Dendro-bates histrionicus *demonstrate the remarkable range of colors and patterns that exist within a single species. These frogs live in the tropical lowlands and mountain rain forests of Ecuador and Colombia.*

Surinam (located on the northern coast of South America), is usually a vivid shade of blue, dotted with black speckles. While the male musters only a "subdued croaking" to attract a mate, Heselhaus says, the female actively courts the male by nudging him and stroking his back—which the male apparently finds "impossible to resist."

The shy green-and-black–banded *Dendrobates auratus* of Costa Rica and Panama, which grows somewhat larger than other species (up to 2.375 inches or 59 mm), has been identified in at least fifteen different color schemes. This frog is particularly fond of cocoa plantations, according to Heselhaus, where rotting

fruit attracts insects at harvest time. In recent years, *D. auratus* has been successfully introduced to the Hawaiian islands.

Dendrobates histrionicus, like many of its counterparts, also sports an array of bright colors, from chocolate-brown, beige, and red to reticulated yellow and black, along with spots or bands of red, green, yellow, or white. (In the so-called "bull's-eye" phase, the frog is black with bright orange spots.) Averaging about 1.50 inches (38 mm) in length, this species lives on the forest floor of tropical lowlands and rain forests of western Colombia and Ecuador. In captivity, females have been observed transporting unfertilized eggs to bromeliad vases as a source of food for surviving tadpoles.

"A frog that feeds its young!" rhapsodizes Heselhaus. "This was indeed a sensational discovery, showing what highly evolved forms of parental care such a tiny species of frog was capable of."

The Colombian *Dendrobates lehmanni*, which crossbreeds with *D. histrionicus*, has wide alternating red-and-black or red-and-white bands across its body. (Extreme variability in their patterns and colors has led frog authority Christopher Mattison to declare, "No two are alike.") The call of the male reportedly resembles the noisy quacking of ducks.

Another Colombian species, *Phyllobates bicolor*, is one of the most toxic of all dart-poison frogs. Native Americans imitate the male's peeping call by whistling and tapping their cheeks with their fingers, according to Gerald Wood; frogs that answer the call are easily located and caught. Nonetheless, even the natives are reluctant to handle the frogs without leaves to protect their hands from contact. Growing to only 1.50 inches (38 mm), these frogs are usually red, orange, or yellow, with black undersides and legs.

Other intriguing family members include the "rocket frogs" (*Colostethus*) of Central and South America—also known as "false dart-poison frogs," since they are nontoxic—which grow only about 0.625 inches (17 mm) long and "zip about as fast as rockets," according to Heselhaus, and *Epipedobates tricolor*, which secretes alkaloids that may prove even more effective than morphine as an anesthetic. As more species of dart-poison frogs are discovered each year, researchers hope that their unusually potent toxins will prove valuable in the fight against humanity's most debilitating diseases.

Dart-poison frog
The female Phyllobates vittatus, *a dart-poison frog that lives in lowland forests of Costa Rica, strokes the male's back before depositing a clutch of eggs on a bromeliad leaf. The male then fertilizes the eggs on the leaf and guards them for roughly two weeks, before transporting the tadpoles on his back to small pools of water.*

Dart-poison frog
Scientists have discovered that the dart-poison frog Epipedobates tricolor *secretes a substance that may prove even more effective than morphine when used by humans as a pain-killer or sedative.*

Native Americans imitate the peeping call of the male *Phyllobates bicolor* by whistling and tapping their cheeks with their fingers; frogs that answer the call are easily located, caught, and used for poison.

Greenhouse Frog
Eleutherodactylus planirostris planirostris

*T*he greenhouse frog is one of North America's tiniest frogs, typically reaching only 0.625–1.25 inches (17–31 mm) in length.

Greenhouse Frog
Eleutherodactylus planirostris planirostris

From the largest genus of amphibians in the world (420-plus species) comes one of North America's tiniest frogs: the greenhouse frog (*Eleutherodactylus planirostris planirostris*), a relatively recent immigrant to Florida from the West Indies.

Aside from its miniature size—0.625–1.25 inches (17–31 mm)—this diminutive frog fascinates observers because of its unusual breeding process: Eggs are laid on land, not in water, without a protective bubble mass, and the baby frogs hatch directly from the eggs, bypassing the free-swimming tadpole stage altogether. Actually, the embryo does undergo a tadpole-like stage—visible if an egg is examined closely—but it remains inside the thick membrane of the egg, where it develops into a fully developed froglet with a short tail before hatching. The greenhouse frog is one of only two U.S. frogs east of Texas that lays its eggs on land—a trait common among the nest-building frogs of tropical America, southern Africa, and Australia.

When the tiny greenhouse froglet is ready to emerge from its protective shell, it uses an egg tooth (similar to that found on fledgling birds and some reptiles) on the tip of its snout. This is a "true tooth," Cochran reports, although it performs but a single function and is shed not long after the hatching.

These minute hatchlings—only 0.20 inches (5 mm) long—"in size and actions resemble tiny fleas," Porter observes. "To watch these almost microscopic froglets is a thrilling and awe-inspiring experience. They are so tiny, and so bold." In fact, the froglets are near-perfect replicas of their parents—except for their tails, which soon disappear.

The female greenhouse frog lays her eggs singly under plant debris, often under a flowerpot in a greenhouse or directly on the ground beneath the shelter of a board or log. If suitable cover is not available, Olive Goin discovered, the mother may cover her eggs by kicking dirt on them.

Porter once followed the development of several egg clusters and noticed an adult frog squatting next to the cluster. "It makes me inclined not to dismiss the possibility that the greenhouse frog, like its relative the barking frog, offers its eggs certain, if minute, parental care," he concluded.

Greenhouse frogs come in two pattern phases—striped (with two lines down the back, one on each side) and mottled (or, in rare instances, a combination of the two). The coloration on the frog's back is generally some shade of brown—usually tan or reddish—with a pale belly and prominent scarlet-red eyes.

On the Florida peninsula, where these immigrants are now well established, the frogs live in leaf mold and moist litter near human habitation (favoring greenhouses, garden beds, and dumps) or in moist wooded areas, hardwood hammocks, and the burrows of gopher tortoises. The nocturnal frogs are most often seen during or after rains, when moisture is plentiful and humidity is high. (Floridians report they are able to coax the tiny frogs from their hiding places by turning on lawn sprinklers at night.)

Goin likens the vocalization of the male greenhouse frog to the "twittering of a baby duckling," and other experts characterize the calls as birdlike chirps, faint musical cheeps, or short whistling notes.

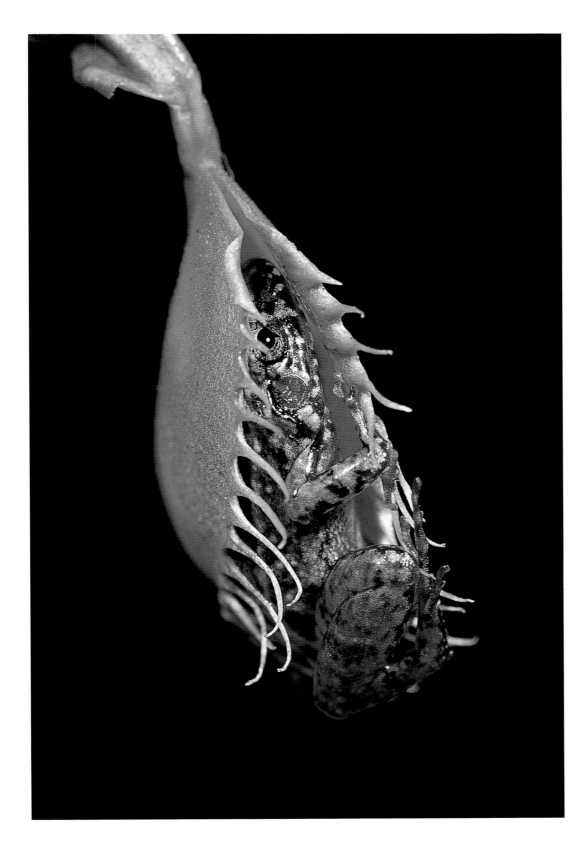

*T*he greenhouse frog is one of only a few U.S. frogs that lay their eggs on land—a trait common among the nest-building frogs of tropical America, southern Africa, and Australia.

Greenhouse frog
A greenhouse frog struggles to extricate itself from a carnivorous Venus flytrap. These tiny tropical frogs, introduced to Florida and Louisiana from Cuba, lay their eggs on land instead of in water, often beneath greenhouse flowerpots or in decaying vegetation and damp leaf litter.

113

Glass Frog
Centrolenella fleischmanni

Glass Frog
Centrolenella fleischmanni

Examining a glass frog through its translucent, seemingly transparent skin is like receiving a lesson in anatomy: From the underside, you can view the bones, muscles, intestines, and other organs—including the beating heart. Sometimes referred to as ghost frogs or glass tree frogs, these amphibians comprise a genus with three families and some sixty-four species, most of which live in tropical rain forests or montane zones (cool, moist upland slopes below the timberline) in Central and South America, from Mexico to Brazil and Argentina.

Delicate, thin-limbed, and equipped with large suction disks on their toes, glass frogs are generally bright green or yellow-green (looking "a bit like a lime Jello mold," one naturalist suggests), sometimes speckled with light dots. Their eyes are quite small, set back against the head, with a silver iris and horizontal pupil. Once classified as tree frogs because of their arboreal habits and large suction pads, the *Centrolenella* family of frogs and their relatives have a distinct hook or bony spine visible on the upper arm near the shoulders. Some scientists believe that males use this hook as a weapon to defend their territory against encroaching males and perhaps inflict wounds on other frogs. In females, the hook is internal or absent altogether.

Centrolenella fleischmanni, sometimes referred to as Fleischmann's frog, is a small species, averaging about 0.75 inches (19 mm), found in the montane forests of Costa Rica, where it apparently has some difficulty adjusting to changing temperatures. According to Duellman and Trueb, the advertisement call of this glass frog is a series of "long-range courtship peeps" interspersed among "soft mews."

Females deposit unpigmented eggs on the undersides of fronds and other leaves (most species of glass frogs lay their eggs on the upper surfaces or tips of foliage) overhanging streams; when the larvae hatch, they fall into the water. According to Susan Jacobson, the male Fleischmann's frog engages in a rather unusual form of paternal behavior: Not only does he sit with the clutch, after the female leaves, to guard the eggs from would-be predators, he also rotates on top of them and urinates bladder water to keep the eggs from drying out. While guarding the clutch, some male glass frogs will eat any eggs damaged by parasites to control the spread of disease and protect the healthy remaining eggs.

Glass large-eyed frog
The glass large-eyed frog Leptopelis bocagii *looks like frosted glass or lime Jell-O when seen from above.*

114

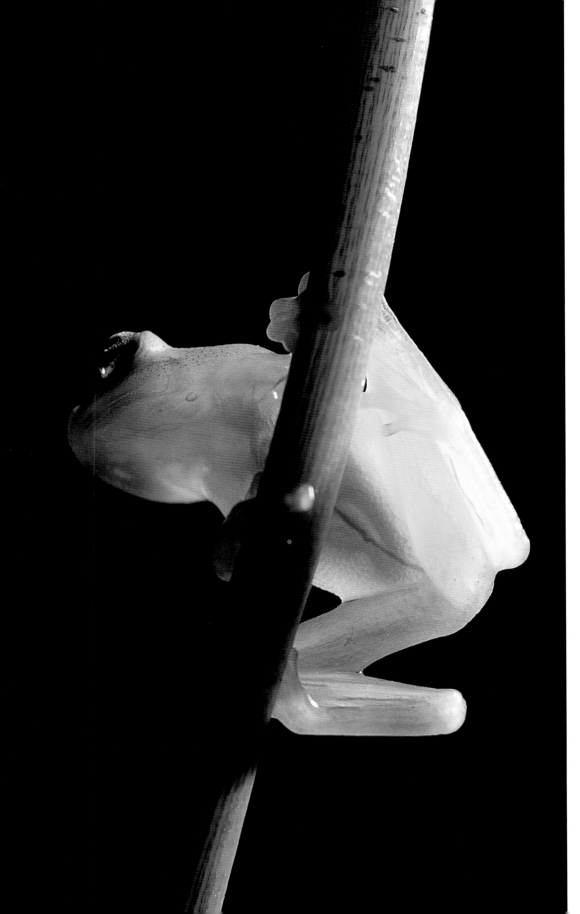

The glass frog has a distinct hook or bony spine visible on the upper arm; it's believed that males use this hook as a weapon to defend their territory.

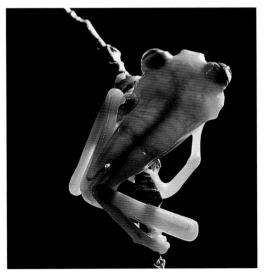

Top: Glass large-eyed frog
The glass large-eyed frog Leptopelis bocagii *is delicate, thin-limbed, and equipped with large suction disks on its toes.*

Left: Glass frog
One of many species of glass frogs, the small, delicate Centrolenella fleischmanni, *or glass tree frog, has translucent skin that offers a fascinating glimpse of its internal organs. Viewed from the underside, this frog's beating heart is clearly visible.*

115

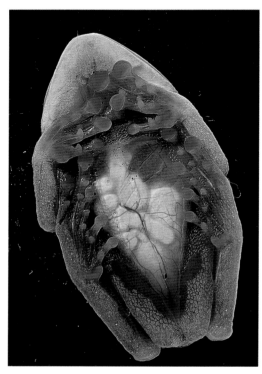

Glass large-eyed frog
A lesson in frog anatomy. Looking at a glass large-eyed frog from the underside through its translucent skin, you can view the bones, muscles, intestines, and other organs—including the beating heart.

Glass large-eyed frog
The outline of the glass large-eyed frog's skeletal system is visible when the frog is lit from below.

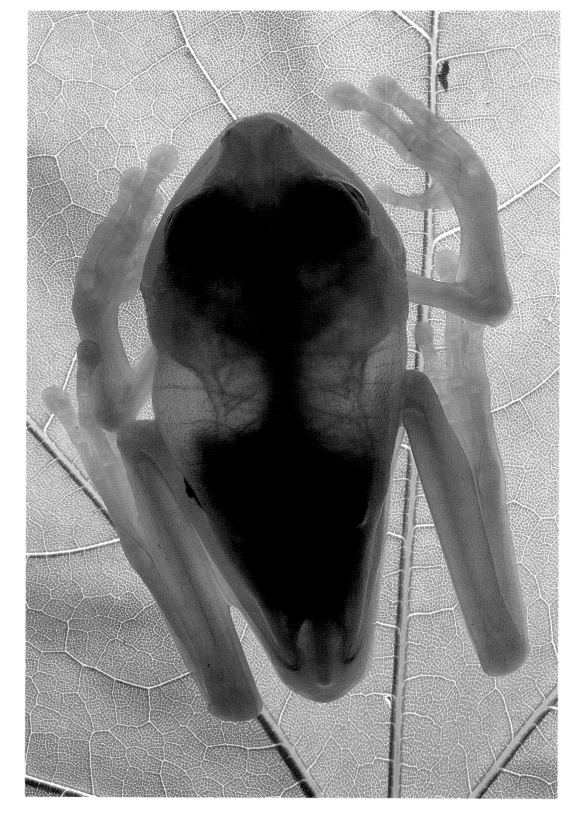

Argentine Horned Frog
Ceratophrys ornata

Youngsters liken it to Jabba the Hutt in *Return of the Jedi*; pet-shop owners call it the "Pac-Man" frog; and most South Americans simply refer to it as *escuerzo,* "the toad." The Argentine horned frog (*Ceratophrys ornata*) acquired these nicknames because of its odd physical characteristics: a massive body (up to 7 inches, or 175 mm, long), an enormous mouth, and two menacing "horns" that jut out over its eyes. In truth, the horn-like appendages are only upper eyelids—but the image this bulky beast manages to project is one of downright unfriendliness, which happens to match its real-life personality.

A native of Uruguay, Brazil, and northern Argentina, the Argentine horned frog has been characterized variously as aggressive, pugnacious, and belligerent. It does not hesitate to use sharp teeth on its upper jaw or bony structures on its lower jaw against approaching enemies; in fact, it will jump right toward them in a most unfroglike manner.

"More than one collector has been bitten painfully as he extended a hand to capture the horned frog," Smyth says. "Once this frog has a hold, he is as difficult to shake loose as a snapping turtle or a bulldog, for he hangs on as tenaciously as they do."

The jaws of this species open and shut "with lightning rapidity" and an "audible snap," Gadow reports, and some South Americans believe that a grazing horse will die if bitten on the lip by a horned frog. While the "fangs" of this frog harbor no poison, "from what we know," Maurice and Robert Burton declare, "it is easy to believe that it would not hesitate to snap at a horse." Furthermore, they add, "its teeth might leave a wound that becomes septic, so causing the death of a horse."

Argentine horned frog
The Argentine horned frog spends much of its time partially buried in loose soil or concealed in leaves and grasses, waiting to ambush prey that strays into range. Dubbed the "Pac Man" frog because of its large mouth, this frog is quite belligerent and will bite humans with its sharp teeth.

Actually, the horned frog has no need to take a chunk out of an Argentine stallion; instead, it buries itself in the ground or among leaf litter, exposing only its bulging eyes, and waits for a manageable-sized meal (say, a mouse, lizard, frog, bird, or large insect) to amble into range. If there isn't enough grass around to blend in with the frog's garish skin coloration—a mix of green, yellow, and red with blotches of brown or black—it may toss lumps of earth on its warty back to enhance the camouflage. The width of a horned frog's mouth, harboring a heart-shaped tongue, sometimes exceeds half the length of its body.

These daytime ground-dwellers bear a striking resemblance to the African bullfrog and are in great demand among pet hobbyists because of their grotesque ap-

Argentine Horned Frog
Ceratophrys ornata

A frican bullfrogs are voracious eaters, consuming not only the usual insect fare, along with earthworms, small reptiles, and amphibians, but also chickens, ducks, and small mammals.

pearance. But solitary confinement is essential for specimens, Mattison observes, because of their cannibalism and "indiscriminating appetites."

The natural habitat of the horned frog includes tropical rain forests as well as prairie pampas regions, where they burrow into the ground during the dry season and slough off a cocoon-like parchment that retains mucous secretions and other moisture. When the rainy season arrives, males emerge from their underground burrows and spawn in jungle pools and small lagoons, advertising their presence to prospective mates with a sound characterized as a "bovine-like" bellow.

African Bullfrog
Pyxicephalus adspersus

The African bullfrog may be better known by its nickname—the "pyxie" frog, a corruption of its scientific name, *Pyxicephalus adspersus*—but one glimpse of this behemoth will convince an observer that it is anything but a pixie.

Although the African bullfrog is not the world's largest frog (that title is held by the goliath frog), it nonetheless achieves gargantuan size: Males grow up to a whopping 9.5 inches (238 mm). In an exception to the general rule, females attain only about half the size of males. Variously described as enormous, grotesque, and gluttonous, this inhabitant of tropical Africa south of the Equator has been dubbed "the frog king of exotic eating" by Kathryn Phillips, and William Duellman calls it "a walking stomach."

These voracious eaters consume not only the usual insect fare, along with earthworms, small reptiles, and amphibians, but also tackle chickens, ducks, and small mammals (mice are a favorite diet in captivity, although too many can cause a weight problem or even death). In captivity, these frogs bury themselves up to their eyes in moss or leaf litter and lunge at approaching prey. Their enormous mouths are equipped with three tooth-like projections in the lower jaw, which can inflict a nasty bite. One of the more bizarre accounts of their appetite involves a zookeeper in South Africa who nabbed an African bullfrog "after it swallowed 17 baby spitting cobras in a reptile enclosure," Phillips recounts. "The snakes were noticeably longer than their attacker, but being outsized and outnumbered didn't discourage the frog."

In their native habitat of dry, semi-desert grasslands, savannas, and steppes, African bullfrogs burrow beneath the

African bullfrog
The male African bullfrog, or "pyxie frog" (a variation on its scientific name, Pyxicephalus adspersus*), aggressively defends its territory against intruders. During dry periods, these large frogs estivate underground in cocoonlike layers of skin, emerging during the rainy season to woo females with their loud bellowing call.*

ground, using the sharp tubercles on their powerful hind legs, and estivate for long periods in cocoons of several dozen layers of parchmentlike skin. During the rainy season, they emerge from their burrows to breed in temporary ponds. Attracted by the loud, deep bellows of the males, females arrive at the pools and lay three thousand to four thousand eggs after mating. The eggs hatch swiftly (sometimes in only two days), and the tadpoles metamorphose quickly, developing into frogs in less than three weeks.

Males of the species exhibit a rare parental interest in their young, protecting the eggs and emergent tadpoles from harm and lunging aggressively at would-be predators (and photographers who get too close). Paradoxically, these bullfrogs are also cannibalistic, gobbling down frogs of their own species as well as their own tadpoles.

The African bullfrog is occasionally confused with the South American horned frog (both have big mouths and share a taste for rodents), but, despite reputations for aggressiveness and jaws like steel traps, they do not look alike. The olive-green bullfrog has large, protruding eyes (but no horny projections, like the South American frogs), a yellow to orange throat, and raised ridges on its back; younger specimens may have pale dorsal stripes. In Africa, people regard these massive frogs as a real delicacy.

Tomato Frog
Dyscophus guineti
The tomato frog of Madagascar is aptly named: The three to six species belonging to the genus *Dyscophus* are shiny red, orange-red, or reddish brown and look

Tomato frog
Although the tomato frog of Madagascar is prized as a pet for its remarkable resemblance to a ripe tomato, its trademark orange-red skin color often fades among successive generations bred in captivity.

like ripe tomatoes. They are so prized as terrarium pets, however, that many generations have been bred in captivity as pet-shop specimens and, as a result, are now considerably paler than those in the wild.

Herpetologists concede they still know relatively little about tomato frogs, despite their "glamorous" contemporary image as "hot" vegetable (or berry) look-alikes. These frogs range from about 3–4.50 inches (75–113 mm) and have relatively flat heads, horizontal pupils, partially webbed hind feet, and no adhesive disks on their toes. They live in ditches and streams in the Antongil Bay region and coastal areas of northeastern Madagascar, a large island in the Indian Ocean off Africa's southeast coast.

Tomato Frog
Dyscophus guineti

119

The Senegal running frog doesn't hop or jump like an ordinary frog—it walks or runs on short, thin hind legs.

Senegal running frog
The ground-dwelling Senegal running frog inhabits the savannas and open grasslands of Africa, where it favors running to hopping. Herpetologists liken the male's explosive call to the sound of a cork popping out of a bottle.

Senegal Running Frog
Kassina senegalensis

Senegal Running Frog
Kassina senegalensis

The Senegal running frog doesn't hop or jump like an ordinary frog—it walks or runs on hind legs that are conspicuously short and thin. One of about twenty species of striped African running frogs, *Kassina senegalensis* is not restricted to the west African nation of Senegal but is also found throughout the savannas and open grasslands of eastern and southeastern Africa.

These little frogs (about 1.50 inches, or 38 mm, in length) are handsomely though variably patterned, with three or five rich-brown stripes on a light olive-green or silver background, one stripe running from the tip of the snout to the rear and the others starting near the eyes. Occasionally, spots or oval blotches are also visible. The frog's skin is smooth, its pupils vertical, and its fingers and toes webbed only slightly, if at all, with rounded toes but no adhesive disks.

During extended periods of dryness, these frogs estivate in burrows which they dig into the mud; during the winter rainy season, they frequent swamps, bogs, flooded plains, and temporary pools of water. The call of the male Senegal running frog is remarkably loud and distinctive, Massimo Capula reports, resembling "an escaping bubble of air" or the popping sound of "a cork being removed from a bottle." Females lay their eggs singly in standing water or attach them to aquatic vegetation. After the tadpoles hatch, they are "always hungry," according to Cochran, and they gnaw on the stems and leaves of reeds and other available plants. The adults are nocturnal and feed on a variety of invertebrates.

Harlequin Frog
Atelopus flavescens

Despite its smooth skin, slender torso, dazzling colors, and highly toxic skin secretions—which cause frequent confusion with dart-poison frogs—the pink-bellied harlequin frog of Central and South America is actually a toad. Like its fellow forty-four-plus species of harlequin frogs, this frog has a Bidder's organ—a rudimentary reproductive gland found in male true toads that develops into functioning ovaries if the testicles are removed.

Toad status and testicles aside, these frogs interest herpetologists and collectors alike because of their unusually long bouts of amplexus, their exceptionally brief larval hatching periods, and their transsexual calling talents.

To insure successful mating, male harlequin frogs sometimes clasp a female "early in the season" and "guard her until she is ready to spawn," Halliday and Adler report. (One pair set an all-time record by remaining in the amplexus position for 125 days.) Females lay short strands of unpigmented eggs in temporary rain pools or moving water, and the eggs float on the surface for a mere twenty-four hours before the tadpoles hatch. According to Duellman and Trueb, *Atelopus* tadpoles develop large oral disks that help them to survive in torrential streams by adhering to rocks. These disks are reportedly so efficient that scientists sometimes have to pry the "torrent tadpoles" off rocks in order to observe them.

At the time of breeding, both sexes are able to call, making harlequin frogs one of only a few species in which the female also has a voice. Their call is quite musical, Cochran says ("two ringing, bell-like notes followed by a descending trill"), more like the call of a bird than the song of a frog. Specimens in captivity some-

times make another sound, she says, a chirping noise that sounds like young turkeys.

The bright colors and dashing patterns sported by these frogs are absolutely breathtaking: Some species are red with brown markings, others are bright yellow, orange, or brown with black reticulations. According to Mattison, species inhabiting lowland areas have longer legs and are generally more brightly colored than montane species living at higher altitudes—e.g., Andes plateaus and cloud for-

Harlequin frog
Harlequin frogs of Central and South America display bands of dashing colors like those worn by characters in sixteenth-century pantomimes. This pink-bellied harlequin frog is highly toxic; its colorful bands and pink underside likely serve as a warning to predators to keep their distance.

The harlequin frog has highly toxic skin secretions, causing it to be frequently confused with dart-poison frogs.

ests of Ecuador, Colombia, and Peru—which have shorter legs and are more likely to be black or dark gray ("all adaptations to surviving in cold conditions," he explains).

The noses of several species of harlequin frogs look rather peculiar; some snouts are beaklike, while others look like the tips have been cut off. Harlequin frogs prefer to walk rather than hop, and when they feel threatened, they bend their head and legs upwards in the "canoe position" (a trait also exhibited by fire-bellied toads) to display their bright warning colors. However, since these frogs are highly toxic, scientists believe they have relatively few enemies in the wild.

Sedge Frog
Hyperolius puncticulatus

The sedge frog of Africa exhibits an unusual trait (for amphibians) that endears it to many human observers: It will sit on a bank and sunbathe for hours at a time, especially on cool mornings, despite its otherwise nocturnal behavior.

Hyperolius puncticulatus is one of more than 120 species of sedge frogs—small, brilliantly colored frogs transferred from one family to another by scientists who have encountered particular difficulties establishing their taxonomic status. Sedge frogs are found throughout Africa south of the Sahara, ensconced among the rushes and sedge (tufted marsh plants) that grow near the shore of ponds, lakes, rivers, and swamps. The color combinations of sedge frogs vary widely, depending on such variables as geography, temperature, humidity, intensity of light, and even stress. Though primarily decked out in bright greens, yellows, and browns, some sedge frogs also have prominent stripes, spots, or marbled patterns.

Usually found near water, where they thrive on a diet of mosquitoes and gnats, sedge frogs also turn up on agricultural lands and in rain forests of tropical Africa. During the dry season, these frogs retreat into burrows or rocky crevices, where they estivate for months at a time until the rains resume. Sedge frogs may congregate in great numbers, even though each male "regulates" his own small territory, according to Cochran. The male has a metallic-sounding chirp, which serves as a sort of acoustical marking device, but he will resort to physical defense of his territory if provoked.

Unlike some of their relatives, these sedge frogs are not foam or bubble nesters, instead laying their eggs in clumps just above the surface of the water or on leaves of submerged water plants. In captivity, successive generations have begun to evidence more and more signs of genetic degeneration and increasingly high mortality rates.

Sedge frog
The sedge frog, or yellow-spotted reed frog, is a native of coastal Kenya and eastern Africa. It often sunbathes for hours at a time on the shore of a lake, where it hunts mosquitoes and gnats among the water plants.

Shovel-Nosed Frog
Hemisus marmoratus

The shovel-nosed or pig-nosed frogs of tropical and subtropical Africa don't have spades on their hind feet like the spadefoot toads of North America, Europe, and Asia; instead, they have evolved tiny, triangular heads with hardened snouts for headfirst burrowing.

The five species of shovel-nosed frogs, including *Hemisus marmoratus*, are occasionally confused with the spatulate-nosed or casque-headed tree frog because of their elongated snouts, but the latter is an arboreal species and has a head and nose that resemble those of a gecko or a miniature alligator. The habitat of *Hemisus marmoratus* is sub-Saharan Africa, excluding rain forests, Somalia, and northern regions of the Republic of South Africa.

This species is renowned for its singular method of tunneling, Cochran observes. The frog "dives headfirst into the soft soil and uses its piglike snout for digging. The sharp nose is further accented by a very receding underjaw." Although it lives underground, where its diet consists chiefly of termites and ants, it is reputed to be a competent swimmer.

The shovel-nosed frog is a tiny fellow, only about 1.50 inches (38 mm) in length, with green- or yellow-marbled skin patterns set against a background shade of brown. During the breeding season, the female excavates a smooth, spherical passage underground in a bank next to water and lays up to two thousand eggs. Unlike most frogs, however, she remains to brood the eggs, sitting on the clutch in the subterranean chamber until they hatch. When the larvae emerge, she digs a tunnel from her nest to the pool, and the hatchlings "wriggle their way down the passageway" to the pool, Smyth explains,

Shovel-nosed frog
The shovel-nosed frog of tropical Africa has a marbled skin pattern and hardened snout, which it uses to excavate a nesting chamber under the bank of a pool. After her eggs hatch, the female digs a tunnel from the nest to the water, permitting her tadpoles to slide into the pool.

where they undergo their metamorphosis. Should a delay occur after the eggs hatch, researchers have found, the tadpoles can actually survive for a period of up to eighteen days out of water.

Malayan Narrow-Mouthed Toad
Kaloula pulchra

The Malayan narrow-mouthed toad (*Kaloula pulchra*), also called the Chinese painted frog and the Indian bullfrog or ox frog, is an outgoing creature—less shy and secretive than its nine fellow species of *Kaloula* and frequently found in urban areas. This toad not only thrives in city parks and village gardens, it also defiantly enters homes in search of insects.

As its several names suggest, this toad or frog is found throughout Southeast Asia—from southern China to Singapore, Borneo, southern India, and Sri Lanka. Its scientific name derives from its unusual

*S*hovel-nosed frogs have tiny, triangular heads with hardened snouts for headfirst burrowing.

Malayan narrow-mouthed toad
After a heavy rainstorm, the Malayan narrow-mouthed toad, or Chinese painted frog, can be heard bellowing like a bull. This explains its assortment of nicknames, including the Indian bullfrog and the ox frog.

colors—mostly raspberry-pink, with a wide earth-brown stripe or spot on the center of its back and two mustard-yellow bands on either side, separated from the pink flanks by a thin brown border. Occasionally spots appear on the arms and legs.

The shape of this robust toad is as unusual as its colors: While the body is quite plump, the head is small, with large eyes, round pupils, and a short snout. The limbs are short but sturdy, and the back legs are equipped with horny spades for burrowing in damp soil. When threat-ened, the toad inflates its puffball-shaped body to even greater size.

Adult toads measure only 2–3.25 inches (50–81 mm) in length, but their loud ox-like bellows suggest a much larger animal. Males emerge from their burrows after heavy rainstorms and congregate in temporary puddles, sounding off at night to attract mates. Abdominal glands on narrow-mouthed toads secrete a sticky substance that helps males to remain securely attached to females during am-plexus.

Water-Holding Frog
Cyclorana novahollandia

The water-holding frogs of Australia are celebrated for their ability to retain significant quantities of water during periods of drought—a curious gift that has been exploited for centuries by desert-dwelling aborigines.

As the Australian herpetologist Raymond Hoser explains it, "Aboriginals in desert areas . . . dug up water-engorged frogs in dried-up ponds, placed the rear of a frog in their mouth, and squeezed water from the frog." Since the bladders could store as much as half the frog's total body weight in water, the natives who knew how to locate these creatures several feet underground were tapping a source of moisture that not only could quench their thirst but also save their lives.

On a continent where more than half of the land mass receives only 10 inches (250 mm) of rain per year or less—and where some areas receive less than 5 inches (125 mm) annually—the burrowing and water-conserving habits of these frogs have provided an evolutionary advantage. Digging down 3 feet (0.90 meters) below the surface, water-holding frogs create a "skin bag" or cocoon by sloughing off the outer layer of their skin (except at the nostrils). Water accumulates between the frog's skin and the cocoon, but the skin bag inhibits evaporation. The frog remains "in a torpid state," Halliday and Adler explain, eating nothing—until the next rainstorm, when it resurfaces to feed and replenish its water supply.

At least seven species of water-holding frogs are found in Australia, many of them glimpsed only after sudden tropical thunderstorms when they are scrambling to find water to breed in. At times, drought-stricken areas are so inundated with these frogs that local automobile traffic is held up. In one famous incident, the transcontinental railway was actually halted in central Australia during one spring migration, when "so many frogs were squashed on the rails that the train wheels were unable to gain traction on the slippery surface," Halliday and Adler recount.

The northeastern water-holding frog (*Cyclorana novahollandia*) is a fairly large, greenish gray species, growing up to 4 inches (100 mm) long and resembling a toad because of its stout front legs, plump hind legs, and warty skin. It is an "opportunistic feeder," according to Hoser, that primarily eats insects but also consumes geckoes and other frogs if available. In the rain forests of northeastern Australia it may remain active throughout the entire

Water-Holding Frog
Cyclorana novahollandia

Water-holding frog
During periods of prolonged drought, the Australian water-holding frog burrows underground and creates a cocoon to prevent evaporation; after a heavy rain, they emerge and migrate to water in large numbers. On one occasion, so many frogs were squashed on Australia's transcontinental rail line that the wheels of a train lost their traction on the slippery surface.

Red-banded crevice creeper
The African red-banded crevice creeper has a smooth, rubbery skin with zebra-like stripes of red and black. The aposematic, or warning, function of these vivid markings is to alert potential enemies to the copious skin secretions, which can inflame human hands and kill other frogs.

*T*he red-banded crevice creeper has something altogether rare in frogs: a neck. Not only can it move its neck, it can also turn its head from side to side.

year, often squatting in a pool of water for hours at a time with only its nostrils exposed to avoid predators.

Another species of water-holding frog, *Cyclorana cultripes*, tends to exhibit "a rather nervous disposition," according to Australian frog expert M.J. Tyler. "When you reach to pick one up, it commonly opens its mouth wide, screams piercingly, and simultaneously jumps absolutely vertically high into the air, to fall in a heap on the ground where it had been sitting."

Red-Banded Crevice Creeper
Phrynomerus bifasciatus
Throughout the open lowlands of Somalia and Zaire to the Republic of South Africa lives a beautiful red-and-blackstriped frog that goes by several names: the red-banded crevice creeper, the African walk-

ing frog, and the banded rubber frog. Although not a tree frog, *Phrynomerus bifasciatus* has expanded toepads and is an agile climber, often found on the stumps of banana trees, on rocks and walls, and inside termite mounds.

Aside from its shiny zebra-like stripes and rubbery skin, this striking African species has achieved notoriety for its foul-smelling secretions (known to cause rashes on human skin) and for something altogether rare in frogs: a neck. The red-banded crevice creeper not only can move its neck, it can also turn its head from side to side.

According to South African herpetologist Vincent Wager, the crevice creeper usually walks or runs rather than jumps; when feeling threatened, it digs into the ground, rear end first. Growing to about 2.50 inches (63 mm) in length, the crevice creeper usually spends the day in a burrow, emerging primarily (but not exclusively) at night to hunt for food. To listeners, the voice of the male sounds like a shrill whistle, a loud trill, or a high-pitched purr.

"One evening while in Zululand, I became aware of an increasing volume of melodious sound drifting on the winds of a torrential and drying storm," Wager recalls. Perched on reedy vegetation in shallow water were "hundreds of red-banded performers in this incredible concert, and what was most unusual was that this chorus consisted of one frog noise only."

When swimming, these males inflate their vocal sacs and float from one tuft to another, using all four legs, Wager reports. To cover longer distances, however, they position their front legs down the sides of their body and kick forcefully with their hind legs.

Golden Mantella
Mantella aurantiaca

The golden mantella of Madagascar is an alchemist's dream come true: a frog that actually appears to have been transformed into gold. Curiously, it is not alone—the male golden toad (*Bufo periglenes*) of Costa Rica's Monteverde Cloud Forest Reserve (last sighted in 1988) and the Panamanian golden frog (*Atelopus zeteki*) also look like they might have been cast in an alchemist's laboratory.

The golden mantella (*Mantella aurantiaca*) relies on its bright orange coloration not to make itself attractive to other animals but, rather, to ward them off. For years, scientists classified mantellas as members of the dart-poison genus *Dendrobates*; their brilliant golden-orange hue, however, was explained as mimicry—a false warning for predators to keep their distance. At least two species of dart-poison frogs sport similar colors: *Phyllobates bicolor*, which is red, orange-red, or yellow, and *Dendrobates auratus*, which glows with a metallic gold sheen and bands of green. Recent anatomical comparisons, however, indicate that the golden mantella is more closely related to "true frogs," such as the pickerel frog and bullfrog.

Golden mantella
The tiny golden mantella, only about one and a quarter inches long, lives in the tropical rain forests of Madagascar. These brightly colored gold or orange frogs are social animals, congregating in small groups.

Golden Mantella
Mantella aurantiaca

Green mantella
Madagascar's four species of mantellas, including this green mantella, sport a wide range of colors, even between the sexes, making identification difficult. Some scientists believe that fertilization of eggs is internal and that amplexus simply stimulates the female to discharge her eggs.

*T*he mantella's coloring may be a form of mimicry of colorful poisonous frogs, a warning for predators to keep their distance.

The golden mantella is a tiny frog, measuring just 1.25 inches (31 mm) in length, with short legs and distinct adhesive disks on its fingers and toes. Primarily a ground-dwelling resident of tropical rain forests, it is usually found under leaves or logs on the jungle floor or climbing in low-hanging branches. Mantellas are social animals, frequently glimpsed in small groups of their own species. The dark horizontal pupils of their eyes offer a stark contrast to their brilliant orange skin color—a living study in Halloween hues.

The male's advertisement call is a chirping sound. Curiously, copulation with females has been known to take place before the female deposits her eggs among damp leaves on the forest floor—suggesting a rare case of internal fertilization.

The golden mantella is one of four species of mantellas found in the montane forests of Madagascar. A second species, the painted mantella (*Mantella madigascariensis*), has something in common with the presumed-extinct golden toad of Costa Rica: The males and females of both species have different colors—a physical characteristic almost unheard of among frogs. The male painted mantella is bluish black, with bright red on its thighs and inside legs and light-blue spots on its belly. The female is a deep black, with light-green spots in front of its limbs and leg markings similar to those of the male.

*T*he painted mantella boasts a characteristic almost unheard of among frogs: Males and females have different colors. The male is bluish black, with bright red on its thighs and inside legs and light blue spots on its belly. The female is a deep black, with light green spots in front of its limbs.

Painted mantella
The painted mantella is a diurnal (day-active) ground-dweller that produces a birdlike chirping call. Massive destruction of Madagascar's tropical rain forests poses a serious threat to the mantella's continued existence.

Declining Amphibian Populations

ALL OVER THE WORLD, FROM THE UNITED STATES TO AUSTRALIA, FROM SWITZERLAND TO COSTA RICA, from the British Isles to Peru, populations of frogs and toads are in peril. Until recently, however, few people had even heard of declining amphibian populations, and herpetologists themselves do not agree on the seriousness of the frogs' plight.

In the past ten years alone, the golden toad and gastric brooding frog have disappeared completely and are presumed extinct, and "almost one-third of North America's eighty-six species of frogs and toads appear to be in trouble," science writer Emily Yoffe concluded in late 1992. The Wyoming toad (population fifty) and the Houston toad (population under ten thousand) are among America's "most endangered" animal species, according to the California Academy of Sciences, and the golden coqui and the Puerto Rican crested toad are considered "threatened." In 1994, California added the Colorado River toad, Yosemite toad, foothill yellow-legged frog, mountain yellow-legged frog, cascades frog, spotted frog, leopard frog, tailed frog, and Western spadefoot toad to its list of protected animals; elsewhere, agencies in other states determine which species of animals are off limits and which can be hunted—or should be safeguarded.

"I believe," naturalist Edward Hoagland says, "that those of us who care about bears and frogs haven't much time left to write about them, not just because—among the world's other emergencies—a twilight is settling upon them, but because people are losing their capacity to fathom any form of nature except, in a more immediate sense, their own."

Almost one-third of North America's eighty-six species of frogs and toads appear to be in trouble.
—Science writer Emily Yoffe

Gray tree frog
Habitat destruction, water pollution, pesticides, and exposure to increased ultraviolet radiation are taking their toll on amphibian populations around the world. Some frogs, such as the gray tree frog silhouetted here on a redbud leaf, are not threatened at present, but other species are endangered or already extinct.

Water snake eating American toad
Frogs and toads play an important role in the food chain, consuming enormous quantities of insects and, in turn, being eaten by snakes, turtles, birds, small mammals, and man. This American toad was chased by a water snake for some distance along the bank of a creek before it was eventually caught and eaten.

The twilight of the frogs is not a happy prospect to consider; clearly, human beings must be awakened to the threats posed to these creatures before it's too late. Because most frogs and toads lead a double life—a terrestrial or arboreal existence interrupted by seasonal migrations to water to reproduce—they are twice as likely as other vertebrates to get clobbered. The permeability of their skins makes frogs highly vulnerable to toxins and other threats present in water, on land, and in the atmosphere; as a result, some herpetologists regard frogs as im-

portant "bioindicators" of environmental stress.

Today's amphibian populations, these scientists suggest, may be like the canaries of an earlier era. "Frogs are telling bellwethers of wide environmental change," former park ranger Michael Milstein observes, "like the proverbial canary used to detect invisible but deadly fumes in a coal mine." Such change, of course, may spell impending disaster for humanity as well.

Of the many recognized threats to amphibians, pollution is one of the most serious. "Man is the filthiest animal that has ever trod the face of the earth," Peter Matthiessen quotes a witness before a federal pollution-control panel nearly half a century ago. "Man is ineradicably, utterly filthy. And every great nation in every part of the world has made a colossal mess as it has exploited its way through its own country."

Garbage and sewage, toxic wastes, metal contaminants and residues, pesticides, herbicides, fertilizers, salinity, sulfuric and nitric acids in rain and snowfall generated by automobile exhaust and industrial air pollution—these are some of the chemical agents that kill or deform adult frogs, tadpoles, eggs, and sperm.

Widespread destruction of natural habitats and ecosystems is fatal, too. Clearcut logging and deforestation, including razing of tropical rain forests (home to as many as three-fourths of all species of frogs), urban and suburban development, changes in groundwater levels, draining of wetlands and swamps, damming of rivers, isolation of breeding ponds, and interference with migration and dispersal during the breeding season have all taken a heavy toll. Highway roadkills, overcollection of specimens by the pet trade and scientific supply houses, human consumption of frog legs, fire suppression, grazing by cattle, and predation by introduced gamefish and other species (especially bullfrogs) have also affected frog populations. Natural threats include disease (microparasites, fungi, and viral infections), global warming and other climate imbalances, overheating of waters, drought, and winterkill.

As if these threats weren't enough, researchers in the western United States have now determined that increased exposure of frog eggs to sunlight—i.e., to ultraviolet radiation associated with thinning of the ozone layer—significantly increases the mortality rate of frog eggs. Experimental research by Andrew Blaustein and his colleagues at Oregon State University suggests that increased UV-B radiation—which also causes skin cancer and cataracts in humans—may prove to be a global variable responsible for previously unexplained declines around the world.

"Something is out of balance," warns James L. Vial, former coordinator of the Declining Amphibian Populations Task Force. Adds Duellman: "The loss of so many species not only affects the overall stability of ecosystems but brings to an end evolutionary lineages that have survived for millions of years. The magnitude of such is immeasurable."

But not all herpetologists are convinced frogs are seriously threatened. The problem of "standards of proof" has created a "scientific conundrum," Earl McCoy explains; in short, "basic scientists prefer ignorance to misstatement." Without accurate census data, it is difficult to prove that frog populations are declining; a reliable census of frogs is extremely difficult to come by, however, since frogs are generally secretive and nocturnal, and females attracted to calling males seldom linger more than a day or two before dispersing to parts unknown.

Joseph Pechmann and Henry Wilbur argue that "toxicological literature does not support a general statement that amphibians are a relatively sensitive group." Random fluctuations in population sizes can produce apparent declines, they say, along with sampling error and other measurement problems. "Are these reports playing it safe or crying frog?" they question. "Negative repercussions if these reports are wrong could bring about a backlash in the future."

But who can afford to wait while scientists try to devise ways to conduct head counts of amphibian populations in isolated swamps, jungles, deserts, savannas, and mountain ranges? Anecdotal evidence shared at international conferences and estimates provided by field researchers must be heeded. "The era of leisurely data collection probably has passed," McCoy says. "Ecologists cannot hope for a second chance to do things right."

Herpetologist David Wake now fears that "general environmental degradation"—a combination of some of the factors cited earlier—may be the real culprit. "That's the worst thing," Wake told the *New York Times* in 1992. "Frogs are telling us about the environment's overall health. They are the medium and the message."

If that's the case, it is imperative that human beings accept a greater share of responsibility for their destructive activities and initiate precautions to insure preservation of the world's frogs and toads. States and nations must pass tougher legislation to protect threatened species. Sanctions and heavy fines should be imposed against polluters and developers who flout environmental-impact regulations. A campaign of awareness should be waged to alert citizens, educators, politicians, schoolchildren, and others to the dangers faced by many species of amphibians.

And, ultimately, humans will just have to change their habits. Unless they cultivate what Dr. Albert Schweitzer called a "reverence for life," humans should expect, one day, to find the voices of the night forever stilled.

As Dr. Schweitzer reminded us when he received the Nobel Prize for Peace in 1952: "You don't live in a world all alone."

> *A day will come when, after making progress upon progress, man will succumb, destroyed by the excess of what he calls civilization. Too eager to play the god, he cannot hope for the animal's placid longevity; he will have disappeared when the little Toad is still saying his litany, in company with the Grasshopper, the Scops-owl and the others. They were singing on this planet before us; they will sing after us, celebrating what can never change, the fiery glory of the sun.*
> —Jean Henri Fabre,
> *The Wonders of Instinct,* 1918

Frog Photography

PHOTOGRAPHING FROGS IS UNQUESTIONABLY A CHALLENGE. UNLIKE MAMMALS, FOR EXAMPLE, FROGS are quite small and therefore more difficult to locate. And since most species are nocturnal, emerging only under cover of darkness to seek food or prospective mates, they require perseverance and ingenuity on the photographer's part, as well as some knowledge of their behavior and habits.

"You've got to be willing to go out and listen at the right time of year, and you've got to set up the right equipment," says John Netherton, who took the photographs in this book over a period of roughly twenty-five years. "But your presence can alter the frogs' behavior—tree frogs will be quiet when they hear you approaching—so it really requires a great deal of patience."

John has had to wade chest-deep into southern swamps, lie flat on his stomach in western streams, and sit motionless in eastern forests for hours at a stretch to record some of these species on film. He's had to deal with skittish subjects that have jumped onto his beard and forehead, and he's had to part with a few favorite shoes and boots—sacrificed to thick mud and insatiable swamps.

Although he has experimented with a variety of cameras, lenses, and films over the years, John now prefers to photograph amphibians with a lighter-weight Nikon N90 or Nikon F4 camera. He once relied heavily on an 80-200mm zoom lens and bellows, but today he prefers a 200mm Nikkor micro lens when working back from his subject and a 60mm Nikkor micro lens for working in closer—if the subject permits. He uses two Nikon SB-24 flash units mounted on a flash bracket with the 200mm lens and a Nikon SB-21

The clever men at Oxford
Know all that there is to be knowed.
But they none of them know one half
as much
As intelligent Mr. Toad!
—Kenneth Grahame, The Wind
in the Willows, 1908

Red-eyed tree frog
The inquisitive, bulged-eye look of this red-eyed tree frog is characteristic of the species. Tree frogs are photographer John Netherton's favorite frog subjects, as their personalities and antics are so engaging.

macro Speedlight with the 60mm lens. (This unit has a focus illuminator that offers a source of light for focusing on the subject.) He also uses a biker's headlamp as a light source—an adjustable tilting spotlight that can focus its beam and sometimes "mesmerize" the frog at night. His most recent color-slide films of choice are the fine-grain Kodak Lumiere LPZ-100X and Fuji Velvia RVP 50.

"I usually try to get down on the frog's level," John says, "but if you're wading into a pond or swamp and you've got a battery pack—for faster recycling time—you can really blast yourself. Some of the setups I used to carry could get excruciatingly heavy, and out in the middle of a swamp there are few dry places where you can set down your equipment."

John recalls one episode when he got stuck in mud up to his thighs while walking at night in a soft-bottomed pond. "I could only move my body a millimeter at a time to work each foot out of the mud," he notes. "Bats came swooping in to catch moths attracted to my headlamp. They were swooping within six inches of my face, and I was mesmerized by their acrobatics." He no longer bothers to wear waders into swampy waters (they're harder to

Harlequin frog

move, he says); instead, tennis shoes and shorts are his customary attire.

Tree frogs are John's favorite frog subjects, as their personalities and antics are particularly engaging; gray tree frogs clinging to leaves, for example, photographed from the underside in silhouette, have provided some memorable pictures. A few green tree frogs John kept in a greenhouse adjoining his studio have roused his neighbors at odd hours of the night, but a Costa Rican red-eyed tree frog named Sam proved to be his most endearing subject. (Even former Senator and White House Chief of Staff Howard Baker was quite taken with this frog, and he has made handsome color enlargements of pictures he shot while visiting John and Sam in 1994.)

For many years now, John has impressed observers with his talent for mimicking the trill of an American toad. "With toads," he says, "once they get going, they're so intent. Toads will tolerate a lot more than frogs when they're mating." Although the toads will stop trilling when he first approaches, he finds he can encourage them to resume their advertisement call if he trills right back at them.

Sometimes mating toads and frogs aren't the only things he encounters at night. "My office is near a creek in the country," he notes, "and I like to go out after sunset in the spring with a flashlight in search of frogs and toads. One night I got there and saw a water snake eating a toad—but the light agitated the snake, and he released the toad. I kept going back, and, about ten nights later, I saw a toad that was half-way down."

One of the most unusual photos in this book is a picture of an Oriental fire-bellied toad that captures the beauty of the vivid orange belly with black spots. "The only way to photograph this was

from underneath," John explains, "so I put a glass aquarium up at a high level outside and mounted two flashes underneath. My camera was under the tank, and I cut a hole in black posterboard for the lens to protrude through; this prevented reflection from the camera or myself. I took the picture on a sunny day, with clouds drifting overhead and blue sky."

To photograph a bullfrog mid-jump, John asked A. Kenneth Olson of St. Paul, Minnesota, to construct a setup with high-speed strobe lights powered by a motorcycle battery. Three strobe heads were mounted on separate light stands about 10 feet from the frog and pointed in its direction. When the bullfrog jumped, it broke a photocell beam and triggered a single exposure at 1/10,000 of a second—a process that was repeated several times to create the sequence of pictures.

John has photographed many generations of wood frogs laying eggs in the same rain-filled potholes of a remote Tennessee back road, and he annually visits one pond where he sees "hundreds of thousands" of frog eggs every spring. A resident community of red-spotted newts fond of gorging themselves on these eggs has presented some unique photo opportunities, with a portable aquarium briefly holding the eggs and newts.

Some of the specimens John has handled have exuded sticky secretions, but when he photographed dart-poison frogs, he determined to give them plenty of room. "Actually," he explains, "on first encounter I found that if you approach too close, they get agitated. Too much stress can trigger toxic secretions . . . and then the frogs seem to get groggy.

"You should never put the taking of the photos," he concludes, "over the well-being of the animal."

Bibliography

Albert, Magnus, St. (Albert the Great). *Man and the Beasts*, vol. 47. Translated by James Scanlan. Binghamton, NY: Medieval & Renaissance Texts & Studies, 1987. Originally published c. 1280.

Aristophanes. *Frogs*. Translated from the Greek by R. H. Webb. In *The Complete Plays of Aristophanes,* edited by Moses Hadas. New York: Bantam Books, 1962.

Bainbridge, J.S., Jr. "Frogs That Sweat—Not Bullets, But a Poison for Darts." Photographs by Robert Noonan. *Smithsonian,* January 1989: pp. 70–76.

Bakker, Robert. *The Dinosaur Heresies.* New York: William Morrow, 1986.

Barker, Will. *Familiar Reptiles and Amphibians of America.* New York: Harper & Row, 1964.

Bartlett, R.D. "Ribbitting Sales: Frogs, Toads and Treefrogs in the Home Terrarium." *Pet Product News,* April 1993: pp. 1–4.

Beardsley, Tim M. "Skin of Frog . . . A Newly Revealed Defense Has a Potent Effect Against Microbes." *Scientific American,* vol. 257 (October 1987): pp. 36, 40.

Behler, John L., and King, F. Wayne. *The Audubon Society Field Guide to North American Reptiles and Amphibians.* New York: Alfred A. Knopf, 1979.

Blair, W. Frank. "Amphibians and Reptiles." In *Animal Communication: Techniques of Study and Results of Research,* edited by Thomas A. Sebeok. Bloomington: Indiana University Press, 1968: pp. 289–310.

Blaustein, Andrew R. "Chicken Little or Nero's Fiddle? A Perspective on Declining Amphibian Populations." *Herpetologica,* 50:1 (March 1994): pp. 85–97.

Blaustein, Andrew R., Hoffman, Peter D., Hokit, D. Grant, Kiesecker, Joseph M., Walls, Susan C., and Hays, John B. "UV Repair and Resistance to Solar UV-B in Amphibian Eggs: A Link to Population Declines?" *Proceedings of the National Academy of Sciences,* 91:5 (March 1, 1994): pp. 1791–1795.

Bogert, Charles M. "Amphibians and Reptiles of the World." In *The Animal Kingdom,* vol. 2, book 3, edited by Frederick Drimmer. New York: Greystone Press, 1954: pp. 1189–1390.

Boulenger, George A. *The Tailless Batrachians of Europe,* Parts I and II. New York: Arno Press, 1978. Reprint of Ray Society edition, London, 1897.

Boyle, T. Coraghessan. "Hopes Rise." *Harper's Magazine,* March 1991: pp. 60–65.

Bradley, David. "Amphibians Offer a Taste of Their Own Medicine: Drugs From Frog Skin Secretions." *New Scientist,* September 5, 1992: p. 14.

Bragg, Arthur N. *Gnomes of the Night: The Spadefoot Toads.* Philadelphia: University of Pennsylvania Press, 1965.

Burton, Maurice, and Burton, Robert. *Encyclopedia of Reptiles, Amphibians & Other Cold-Blooded Animals.* London: Octopus Books, 1975.

Capula, Massimo. *Simon & Schuster's Guide to Reptiles and Amphibians of the World,* edited by John L. Behler; translated by John Gilbert. New York: Simon & Schuster/Fireside, 1989.

Caramaschi, Ulisses, da Silva, Helio R., and de Britto-Pereira, Monica C. "A New Species of *Phyllodytes* (Anura, Hylidae) from Southern Bahia, Brazil." *Copeia,* 1992:1: pp. 187–191.

Carmichael, Pete, and Williams, Winston. *Florida's Fabulous Reptiles and Amphibians.* Tampa, FL: World Publications, 1991.

Carr, Archie. *The Everglades.* New York: Time-Life Books, 1973.

Carr, Archie. *A Naturalist in Florida: A Celebration of Eden*, edited by Marjorie Harris Carr. New Haven, CT: Yale University Press, 1994.

Carr, Archie, and Goin, Coleman J. *Guide to the Reptiles, Amphibians and Freshwater Fishes of Florida.* Gainesville: University of Florida Press, 1955.

Coborn, John. *The Proper Care of Amphibians.* Neptune City, NJ: T.F.H. Publications, 1992.

Cochran, Doris M. *Living Amphibians of the World.* Garden City, NY: Doubleday & Co., 1961.

Conant, Roger, and Collins, Joseph T. *A Field Guide to Reptiles and Amphibians: Eastern and Central North America.* 3rd ed. Peterson Field Guide Series. Boston: Houghton Mifflin, 1991.

Cooper, Nancy. "Britons Hop to 'Help a Toad Across the Road.'" *Newsweek,* April 7, 1986: p. 52.

Cowen, Ron. "Jumping Gender: Frogs Change From She to He." *Science News,* vol. 137 (March 3, 1990): p. 137.

Daniels, Cora L., and Stevans, C.M. *Encyclopaedia of Superstitions, Folklore, and the Occult Sciences of the World,* vol. 2. Detroit: Gale Research Co., 1971. Reprint of J.H. Yewdale & Sons edition, Chicago, 1903.

DeGraaff, Robert M. *The Book of the Toad: A Natural and Magical History of Toad-Human Relations.* Rochester, VT: Park Street Press, 1991.

Deuchar, Elizabeth M. *Xenopus: The South African Clawed Frog.* London: John Wiley & Sons, 1975.

Dickerson, Mary C. *The Frog Book: North American Toads and Frogs.* New York: Dover Publications, 1969. Unabridged republication of Doubleday, Page & Co., 1906.

Dillard, Annie. *Pilgrim at Tinker Creek.* New York: Bantam Books, 1974.

Donaldson, Gerald. *Frogs: Their Wonderful Wisdom, Follies and Foibles, Mysterious Powers, Strange Encounters, Private Lives, Symbolism and Meaning.* New York: Van Nostrand Reinhold Co., 1980.

Douglas, Flora. *Eloquent Animals: A Study in Animal Communication.* New York: Coward, McCann & Geoghagen, 1978.

Duellman, William E. *The Hylid Frogs of Middle America,* vols. I and II. Lawrence: University of Kansas Museum of Natural History, 1970.

Duellman, William E. "Reproductive Strategies of Frogs: New Species Continue to be Identified." *Scientific American,* 267:1 (July 1992): pp. 80–88.

Duellman, William E., and Trueb, Linda. *Biology of Amphibians.* New York: McGraw-Hill, 1986.

Elliott, Lang. "The Calls of Frogs and Toads: Eastern and Central North America." Ithaca, NY: NatureSound Studio 1992. Booklet and audiotape.

Evans, William F. *Communication in the Animal World*. New York: Thomas Y. Crowell, 1968.

Farmer, John S., and Henley, W.E. *A Dictionary of Slang and Colloquial English*. London: George Routledge & Sons, Ltd., 1912.

Florida Department of Agriculture. *Bullfrog Farming and Frogging in Florida*. Bulletin No. 56. Tallahassee: Florida Department of Agriculture, January 1952.

Froglog: IUCN/SSC Declining Amphibian Populations Task Force Newsletter. Nos. 1–9.

Frost, Darrel R., ed. *Amphibian Species of the World: A Taxonomic and Geographical Reference*. Lawrence, KA: Association of Systematics Collections, 1985.

Gadow, Hans. *The Cambridge Natural History, Vol. III: Amphibia and Reptiles*, edited by S.F. Harmer and A.E. Shipley. Codicote, England: Wheldon & Wesley, Ltd., 1958. Reprint of Macmillan edition, London, 1901.

Gilmore, Charles W., and Cochran, Doris. "Amphibians." In *Cold-Blooded Vertebrates, Part II*, vol. 8, edited by Charles G. Abbot. New York: Smithsonian Institution Series, Inc., 1938: pp. 161–208.

Goin, Coleman J., and Goin, Olive B. *Introduction to Herpetology*. 2nd ed. San Francisco: W.H. Freeman & Co., 1971.

Goin, Olive B. *World Outside My Door*. New York: Macmillan, 1955.

Halliday, Tim R., & Adler, Kraig, eds. *Reptiles and Amphibians*. All The World's Animals Series. New York: Torstar Books, 1986.

Heselhaus, Ralf. *Poison-Arrow Frogs: Their Natural History and Care in Captivity*. Translated by Astrid Mickz. Sanibel Island, FL: Ralph Curtis Books, 1992.

Heusser, H.R. "Frogs and Toads," "Lower Anurans," and "Higher Anurans," in *Grzimek's Animal Life Encyclopedia*, vol. 5, edited by Bernhard Grzimek. New York: Van Nostrand Reinhold Co., 1974.

Hoagland, Edward. "Unsilent Spring." *Nation*, May 26, 1979: p. 590.

Hoagland, Edward. *Balancing Acts: Essays*. New York: Simon & Schuster, 1992.

Holmes, Samuel J. *The Biology of the Frog*. 4th rev. ed. New York: Macmillan Co., 1934.

Hoser, Raymond T. *Australian Reptiles and Frogs*. Sydney, Australia: Pierson & Co., 1989.

Hunt, John. *A World Full of Animals*. New York: David McKay Co., Inc., 1969.

Hunt, Joni Phelps. *A Chorus of Frogs*. San Luis Obispo, CA: Blake Publishing, 1992.

Ingle, David J., and Hoff, Karin. "Visually Elicited Evasive Behavior in Frogs." *BioScience*, 40:4 (April 1990): pp. 284–291.

Jacobson, Susan Kay. "Frog Feats." *International Wildlife*, May–June 1984: pp. 12–17.

Kiester, A. Ross. "Communication in Amphibians and Reptiles." In *How Animals Communicate*, edited by Thomas A. Sebeok. Bloomington: Indiana University Press, 1977: pp. 519–544.

Krutch, Joseph Wood. "The Contemplative Toad." In *Our Natural World*, edited by Hal Borland. Garden City, NY: Doubleday, 1965: pp. 321–328.

Lee, Albert. *Weather Wisdom*. Garden City, NY: Doubleday, 1976.

Leviton, Alan E. *Reptiles and Amphibians of North America*. New York: Doubleday & Co., 1970.

Lewis, Edwin R., and Narins, Peter M. "Do Frogs Communicate with Seismic Signals?" *Science*, 227:4683 (January 11, 1985): pp. 187–189.

Livermore, Beth. "Amphibian Alarm: Just Where Have All the Frogs Gone?" *Smithsonian*, vol. 23 (October 1992): pp. 113–120.

Lovett, Sarah. *Extremely Weird Frogs*. Santa Fe, NM: John Muir Publications, 1991.

Matthiessen, Peter. *Wildlife in America*. New York: Viking, 1987.

Mattison, Christopher. *The Care of Reptiles and Amphibians in Captivity*. Poole, Dorset, England: Blandford Books, Ltd., 1983.

Mattison, Chris. *Frogs and Toads of the World*. New York: Facts on File, 1987.

McClanahan, Lon L., Ruibal, Rodolfo, and Shoemaker, Vaughan H. "Frogs and Toads in Deserts." *Scientific American*, 270:3 (March 1994): pp. 82–88.

McCoy, Earl D. " 'Amphibian Decline': A Scientific Dilemma in More Ways Than One." *Herpetologica*, 50:1 (March 1994): pp. 98–103.

Mertens, Robert. *The World of Amphibians and Reptiles*. Translated from the German by H.W. Parker. New York: McGraw-Hill, 1960.

Milstein, Michael. "Unlikely Harbingers." *National Parks*, 64:7–8 (July-August 1990): pp. 18–24.

Muir, John. *The Story of My Boyhood and Youth*. Madison: University of Wisconsin Press, 1965.

Muntz, W.R.A. "Vision in Frogs." *Scientific American*, 210:3 (March 1964): pp. 111–119.

Myers, Charles W., and Daly, John W. "Dart-Poison Frogs." *Scientific American*, 248:2 (February 1983): pp. 120–133.

Noble, G.K. *The Biology of the Amphibia*. New York: McGraw-Hill, 1931.

Obst, Fritz J., Richter, Klaus, and Jacob, Udo. *The Completely Illustrated Atlas of Reptiles and Amphibians for the Terrarium*. Neptune City, NJ: T.F.H. Publications, 1988.

Oliver, James A. *North American Amphibians and Reptiles*. Princeton, NJ: D. Van Nostrand Co., 1955.

Passmore, N.I., and Carruthers, V.C. *South African Frogs*. Johannesburg, South Africa: Witwatersrand University Press, 1979.

Pechmann, Joseph H.K., Scott, David E., Semlitsch, Raymond D., Caldwell, Janalee P., Vitt, Laurie J., and Gibbons, J. Whitfield. "Declining Amphibian Populations: The Problem of Separating Human Impacts from Natural Fluctuations." *Science*, vol. 253 (August 23, 1991): pp. 892–895.

Pechmann, Joseph H.K., and Wilbur, Henry M. "Putting Declining Amphibian Populations in Perspective: Natural Fluctuations and Human Impacts." *Herpetologica*, 50:1 (March 1994): pp. 65–84.

Pennisi, Elizabeth. "Pharming Frogs: Chemist Finds Precious Alkaloids in Poisonous Amphibians." *Science News*, 142:3 (July 18, 1992): pp. 40–42.

Peters, Samuel. *The Rev. Samuel Peters' LL.D. General History of Connecticut*, edited by Samuel J. McCormick. New York: Irvington, 1977.

Originally published 1781.

Phillips, Kathryn. "Where Have All the Frogs and Toads Gone?" *BioScience*, 40:6 (June 1990): pp. 422–424.

Phillips, Kathryn. "Frogs in Trouble." *International Wildlife*, 20:6 (November–December 1990): pp. 4–11.

Phillips, Kathryn. *Tracking the Vanishing Frogs: An Ecological Mystery*. New York: St. Martin's Press, 1994.

Phillips, Kathryn. "Weird World of the Frog." *International Wildlife*, March–April 1994: pp. 20–26.

Poinar, George O., Jr. "The Amber Ark." *Natural History,* December 1988: pp. 43–46.

Porter, George. *The World of the Frog and the Toad.* Philadelphia: J.B. Lippincott Co., 1967.

Prince, Roger. "Letters to the Editor: Convergent Chemical Evolution?" *Natural History*, May 1994: pp. 4–5.

Richards, Bill. "Toad-Smoking Gains on Toad-Licking Among Drug Users." *Wall Street Journal*, March 7, 1994: pp. A1, A8.

Riger, Robert. *One Frog Can Make a Difference: Kermit's Guide to Life in the '90s*. New York: Pocket Books, 1993.

Smyth, H. Rucker. *Amphibians and Their Ways.* New York: Macmillan, 1962.

Smith, Whitney. *Flags Through the Ages and Across the World.* New York: McGraw-Hill, 1975.

Stebbins, Robert C. *A Field Guide to Western Reptiles and Amphibians.* 2nd ed. Peterson Field Guide Series. Boston: Houghton Mifflin, 1985.

Storey, Kenneth B., and Storey, Janet M. "Persistence of Freeze Tolerance in Terrestrially Hibernating Frogs after Spring Emergence." *Copeia*, 1987:3 (1987): pp. 720–726.

Storey, Kenneth B., and Storey, Janet M. "Frozen and Alive." *Scientific American*, 263:6 (December 1990): pp. 92–97.

Tanara, Milli Ubertazzi. *The World of Amphibians and Reptiles.* Translated by Simon Pleasance. New York: Gallery Books, 1978.

Tandy, Mills, and Keith, Ronalda. "*Bufo* of Africa." In *Evolution in the Genus* Bufo, edited by W. Frank Blair. Austin: University of Texas Press: pp. 119–170.

Thoreau, Henry David. *The Writings of Henry David Thoreau,* edited by Bradford Torrey. New York: AMS Press, 1968. Originally published 1906.

Travis, Joseph. "Calibrating Our Expectations in Studying Amphibian Populations." *Herpetologica*, 50:1 (March 1994): pp. 104–108.

Twain, Mark. *The Celebrated Jumping Frog of Calaveras County.* American Humorists Series. Upper Saddle River, NJ: Literature House/Gregg Press, 1969. Reprinted from C.H. Webb edition, New York, 1867.

Twain, Mark. *The Autobiography of Mark Twain*, edited by Charles Neider. New York: HarperCollins, 1990. Originally published 1917.

Tyler, M.J. *Frogs.* Sydney, Australia: Collins, Ltd., 1976.

Tyler, M.J. *Australian Frogs.* South Yarra, Victoria, Australia: Viking O'Neil, 1989.

Tyning, Thomas F. *A Guide to Amphibians and Reptiles*, edited by Donald W. and Lillian Q. Stokes. Stokes Field Guide Series. Boston: Little, Brown and Co., 1990.

Wager, Vincent A. *The Frogs of South Africa.* Cape Town, South Africa: Purnell & Sons Pty., Ltd., 1965.

Wagner, Betsy. "Nature's Tropical Medicine Chest: The Amphibian Pharmacy's Princely Riches." *U.S. News & World Report*, November 1, 1993: p. 77.

Wake, David B. "Declining Amphibian Populations." *Science*, vol. 253 (August 23, 1991): p. 860.

Walls, Jerry G. *Jewels of the Rainforest—Poison Frogs of the Family Dendrobatidae.* Neptune City, NJ: TFM Publications, 1994.

Weisburd, Stefi. "Frogs Get the Jump on Microbes." *Science News*, 132 (August 8, 1987): p. 85.

Weisburd, Stefi. "Jump for Joy: Blue Frog Babies." *Science News*, 133:16 (April 16, 1988): p. 247.

Wells, Kentwood D. "The Social Behaviour of Anuran Amphibians." In *Animal Behaviour*, vol. 25, 1977: pp. 666–693.

Wood, Gerald L. *The Guinness Book of Animal Facts and Feats.* 3rd edition. Enfield, Middlesex: Guinness Superlatives Ltd., 1982.

Wright, Albert Hazen, and Wright, Anna Allen. *Handbook of Frogs and Toads of the United States and Canada.* 3rd ed. Ithaca, NY: Comstock Publishing Co., 1949.

Yoffe, Emily. "Silence of the Frogs." *New York Times Magazine*, December 13, 1992: pp. 36–38, 66, 76.

Index

141

David Badger lives in Franklin, Tennessee, with his wife, Sherry, and son, Jeffrey. He is an associate professor of journalism at Middle Tennessee State University and a former film critic for WPLN-FM Public Radio in Nashville and book critic and columnist for the Nashville *Tennessean*. He was born in Wilmette, Illinois, and received his A.B. degree from Duke University, M.S.J. degree from Northwestern University, and Ph.D. from the University of Tennessee. He is the author of *Celebrate the First Amendment*; co-author of *Newscraft*; a contributor to *Free Expression and the American Public*; and editor of five books.

John Netherton, a nature photographer for more than twenty-five years, lives in Nashville, Tennessee, with his wife, Judy; together they have five sons. His work has appeared in *Audubon, Natural History, National Wildlife, Nikon World, Popular Photography, Birder's World,* and *WildBird*, and he writes a regular column for *Outdoor Photographer*. His books include *Radnor Lake: Nashville's Walden*; *A Guide to Photography and the Smoky Mountains*; *Florida: A Guide to Nature and Photography*; *Tennessee: A Homecoming*; *Big South Fork Country* (with Senator Howard Baker); *At the Water's Edge: Wading Birds of North America*; *Tennessee Wonders: A Pictorial Guide to the Parks*; and *Of Breath and Earth: A Book of Days*.

American toads